Sle

Christina Dunhill, Frances Gapper,
Andie Hawthorn, Linda Leatherbarrow,
Helen Sandler, Pushpa Sellers,
Robyn Vinten, Wendy Wallace

SLEEPING ROUGH

Stories of the Night

LIME
TREE

First published in Great Britain 1991
by Lime Tree
an imprint of the Octopus Publishing Group
Michelin House, 81 Fulham Road, London SW3 6RB

A CIP catalogue record for this book
is available from the British Library
ISBN 0 413 45401 0

Phototypeset by Intype, London
Printed and bound in Great Britain
by Cox & Wyman Ltd, Reading, Berks.

The quotation from 'The Monkey' by Isak Dinesen is used
by permission. US publisher Random House, Inc.

Acknowledgements

Andie, Christina, Linda, Pushpa and Wendy
would like to thank Alison Fell
for the enormous contribution she has made
over the last few years to their creative development
as writers.

Many thanks to Mike Wallace.

NIGHT The time between day and day, when darkness prevails, from sunset to sunrise, or from 6.00 p.m. to 6.00 a.m.; the dark end of daylight. *Night-hag*, female demon riding the air at night. *Nightmare*, female monster sitting upon & seeming to suffocate sleeper. *Night-walker*, a prostitute, or an animal that moves about by night. In the *night-watches*, during the anxious, wearisome, wakeful, etc. night. *Night-work*, work done, that must be done, by night.

excerpts from the *Oxford English Dictionary*

These stories reclaim the night as our place to inhabit, explore, imagine. We do many things at night, besides sleeping – make love, feed babies, work in factories and hospitals, hunt as vampires, fear attackers, run mad, suffer pain and loneliness, plan revolutions, read and write books. These fourteen stories result from our meeting once a fortnight, through one summer and one winter.

Contents

The Renunciation

Andie Hawthorn

I decided not to get married.

If Jerry could have understood why perhaps he wouldn't have been so devastated. But I suppose it must have been upsetting for him, standing at the altar waiting, with Panis Angelicus and Ave Maria sung twice over and me not turning up. And while he was waiting, and all his side of the family peeking at their watches, his brother flashing the one with the luminous dials, I was sitting in the black Daimler holding my father's hand, looking out of the window, having a vision of the Blessed Virgin herself, so bright and sharp the colour of that blue, sharp against the blue sky itself; it hurt my eyes to look at her, but I did and so I didn't feel my father's hand over mine and I didn't see the sun and the dust over Kilburn High Road.

We had stopped at the traffic lights when Our Lady beckoned; I just opened the car door and stepped out. I heard my father's voice as I crossed over to the other side of the street: 'Come back, you friggin' little whore!' And then all was bliss and blue, with white blood in my veins instead of red, and I was pure and cold as the driven snow.

Oh Lady, come Lady, come now!

1

Five hours later I was sitting in Conchita's flat with no clue as to how I'd got there and Maeve still in her bridesmaid's dress screaming at me to get the hell out of there, preferably on the first plane to Australia or Marbella because they were after my blood. They'd gone to the reception and had the turkey and ham sandwiches and every scrap of cake, even the marzipan miniatures of me and Jerry in Victorian dress, and the Special Brew and champagne was all drunk and now they were after my blood.

'Jesus, Maeve,' I said, and she said, 'Jesus, Mary, Joseph and all the saints won't help you now, you forgot to take your friggin' Largactil, didn't you?' Then she started ranting on at Conchita about having a friggin' loony for a sister and the dog's life I'd led her since our mother, God love her, passed away and how I should have stayed in the bin where I belonged only no bin would have me.

Conchita didn't have her hearing aid in, but she got the gist of it. She never liked Maeve as much as me anyway. I was always the one she gave the money and sweets to when we came knocking at her door. I could hear Jerry's brother in our flat, through the wall of Conchita's living room, swearing blue murder.

'I'm off,' said Maeve, 'I haven't seen you. Conchita, hide your purse and don't let her out of your sight.'

Conchita just carried on watching *Neighbours* and grinning at me. 'Pretty girl,' she said. 'Preetee. No marry, what for? All day cooki, washi, ironi.'

I went into the bathroom and rummaged around in the cabinet for a packet of Conchita's hair dye. She uses the best brand: Debutante. And the colour she uses is Brazen Hussy which is a good, strong colour of red. I thought that would do the trick. I reckoned they could look for me till their eyes dropped from their sockets, but they'd be looking for a platinum blonde with a sweet kind of face. I'd have to do something about that too. I shut the cabinet door and then I saw her again looking out at me from the mirror, her face so familiar it could have been my own. She spoke my name and it was like I'd never heard it before, the way it should sound.

'Marie,' she said, 'meet me tonight,' and I said, 'Lady, I will, but where?'

'Underneath the lamplight, wait for me at midnight. Don't be afraid. It's all over.' The way she spoke, as though she had all the good things in life piled up waiting for me, as though I could have been her own daughter, flesh, blood and all, made me want to sing out loud. My eyes were smarting with the brightness of her so I squeezed them shut and when I opened them again she was gone.

I had just got all the dye spread evenly over my hair when I heard a hammering on the front door and my father ranting on at Jerry's brother for calling me soft in the head.

'God love him,' I thought, but I reckoned I should get a move on so I climbed out of the bathroom window. I've always been skinny but it was a tight squeeze and my wedding dress got ripped. It was ruined anyway, with splodges of red dye on it like great big drops of blood. Maeve saw me from the window as I was shinning down the drainpipe. I took the bouquet which I'd wedged in behind the sash and threw it up to her. She caught it and may God have mercy on her soul. She's been a good sister to me all these years.

It was still light enough for the kids to be out. There was a group of them smashing bottles when I began to run. They started yelling at me and then I heard my father's voice: 'Come back, you friggin' little whore!' and

I looked over my shoulder and saw him hanging out of Conchita's kitchen window.

Conchita was looking out from the bathroom, laughing fit to split her sides and flapping her hands. I heard her calling, 'Chicky, chicky, chicky!' as I turned the corner. This bird had flown the nest.

I had a job to find somewhere to rinse the Debutante from my hair. In the end I went to the public baths and ran in without paying. I was standing under the shower when the attendant found me, but she couldn't order me out because I had no clothes on.

'Five minutes then,' she said. I think she was tired, it being near closing time.

I decided to ditch the wedding dress. I left it for the woman whose clothes I took while she was having a swim. Perhaps when it's cleaned and mended she will find a use for it. Her clothes are all right but I would have liked something a bit smarter than a tracksuit. Also, it was about four sizes too big for me. Still, the black colour went well with my new hair which turned out better than I could have hoped. I always wanted to stand out in a crowd; to be something a bit special. I'm too shy and that's why I never did, but I wanted to all the same. I found some make-up in the woman's bag. There was money there too, but I didn't take it. I'm not a thief. I used some of her eyeliner, lipstick and rouge. When I looked at myself in the mirror I could have sworn I'd never set eyes on myself before.

I left the baths and headed for Pentonville Road. When I reached Kings Cross I was feeling hungry, having had nothing to eat all day but a boiled egg and that at the crack of dawn, with Maeve going on at me to be sure and take the pills and to stop snivelling and be thankful

4

because Jerry was a good man, though not much to look at and thick as two short planks, surely, to think of taking me on, but that he'd had the fruit and now he could pay the price. I hadn't enjoyed my boiled egg.

I stood outside the Burger Delight opposite the station looking through the window at the good food and smelling the fried onions. A man came out, belching and staggering, carrying two half-pound mega burgers and large fries. It was Jerry, drunk as a bishop. We looked each other full in the face and he didn't know me at all.

'I'm waiting for someone actually,' I said, trying to sound posh as he grabbed hold of my arm. He apologized. He's not a bad man, Jerry, not like his pig of a brother who'd have drawn his flick-knife as soon as look at you.

'She ran out on me,' he slurred. 'Ditched me. I'd have done anything for her.' There were tears in his eyes, and in mine too, at the sorry sight.

'Give us a burger, for the love of God,' I said, and he handed one over.

'You look a bit like her,' he said. 'I'm devastated.' He felt in his back pocket for some change and handed some coins over saying, 'Here, get yourself some chips.' Then he headed off over the main road to the pub on the corner.

I didn't spend the money. I stood there eating the burger and counting out the pennies. I love the chink of coins. I put the seventy-five pence in my tracksuit pocket and listened to the sound of a man somewhere nearby strumming on a guitar and singing country and western.

A woman in a white mini-skirt and black stilettos yelled, 'Don't give up your daytime job!' She was leaning against the window of the Burger Delight, looking very pissed off. She said, 'Fuck this for a burton,' and stubbed her fag out with a pointed heel so that sparks flew from it. She looked at me and I looked back, friendly-like, and she asked me what I was gawping at and I asked her if she was waiting for someone, thinking that maybe she'd been stood up.

She laughed at that and said, 'Yeah, you could say that,' and I laughed too thinking that maybe we'd have a bit of a talk because there's nothing I like better than a bit of good talk and it would help pass the time I had to kill before midnight.

Then she said, 'Christ, I need a hit,' and I said, 'What?' and she said, 'Smack, girl, smack,' and began screwing up her face, sniffing and coughing, so I hit her on the back, good and hard, over and over, the way Maeve does for my father when his chest plays him up and he can't catch his breath to draw on a fag let alone breathe.

I don't know what happened next. I was down on the ground, staring at a crack in the pavement. I was opening my mouth but no breath was coming out or in and there was a pain beating in my stomach like a drum. When I looked up she was gone and a man with spots all over his face, and a moustache, was stood there saying something about girls always fighting and needing a firm hand to keep them in order and asking me where I was from and if I was on the run. I was nodding and he was holding out his hand which had a lot of gold rings on it. He told me to come along with him and I was going to say no when I spotted Jerry's brother coming out of the pub over the road with a broken bottle in his hand, so I got up and walked with the man along Euston Road and down some dark streets while the rain came down.

We got to an estate with flats all facing the one bit of courtyard and most of the lights broken so you had to dance about a bit not to step on the dog-shit and broken glass, and he said, 'Home, sweet home,' and ran up a couple

6

of flights, pulling me along behind him. A girl jumped out
at us, wet from the rain, hair dripping, eyes too, where
she'd been crying.

'Please,' she said, sniffing and screwing her face up like
the woman in the stilettos at Kings Cross.

'Get lost,' said the man. 'No work, no joy. Come back
when you've got your act together.'

We got to his place the next flight up and went inside, him
telling me that he hated time-wasters and wasn't in the
business of taking passengers and he didn't want me
thinking he was a soft touch just because he'd a mind to
do me a good turn. While he was talking I was taking a
look at the gorgeous stuff he had in his front room; real
antique bits by the look of them, with cream and gold
around the edges and red lamps with little tassels around
the shades. He opened up a drinks cabinet on the wall and
told me to choose whatever I fancied. I said a Snowball,
thinking that now I'd most likely be having it off with
him, because that's the way of things once a man gets you
a drink, and if I didn't he'd be thinking I was a time-
waster too. All the time I was sipping at the Snowball, he
was standing by the fireplace, with the coal effect throwing
red lights on his face, smiling and asking me questions
about this and that, me thinking it best to say nothing
and keep on smiling.

He said, 'Are you a good girl or a bad girl?' and I said,
'Good,' thinking it was the truth because for all the times
I'd let Jerry have it off with me in the back of his brother's
car, I'd never enjoyed any of them.

He was about to make a move when there was a knocking at the front door. He said, 'Shit!' and went to open it
and in walked Jerry's brother, effing and blinding about
what a fuck of a day he'd had and if he ever got his hands

7

on a certain little tart he'd gouge her eyes out. Then he sat down in an armchair, threw his shoes off and didn't bother looking at me at all.

'Cheer up,' said the other one, then he took a packet from his trouser pocket and threw it over to Jerry's brother. It was the white sherbet-looking stuff wrapped in a bit of clear polythene that I've seen Maeve stashing in her pocket now and then.

Jerry's brother opened it, dipped his finger in and tasted it. 'This is the business,' he said, smiling all over his nasty face.

'Yeah,' said the other one, 'you done well.' Then he jerked his thumb at me, saying how he reckoned they'd got another nice little earner and all I needed was a bit of breaking in. Jerry's brother looked at me a bit suspicious-like, but mostly bored, saying he'd had enough of stupid tarts for one day and the other one told him not to be a div because business was business, then Jerry's brother switched the telly on and slugged at a bottle of Scotch. I was thinking I'd best creep out while they were both watching when the other one said I was to go in the bed-room and sort some gear out for myself.

There was mirror on every bit of wall in the bedroom and a big one on the ceiling right over the bed. 'I like to see what's going on,' he said, then he opened up one of the mirror doors to the biggest wardrobe you've ever seen and told me to take my clothes off. I said I was scared of catching a chill and he said about how I'd told him I was a good girl and good girls do as they're told and why was I looking so bloody miserable all of a sudden? I said how there was someone I wanted to go and meet and he said never mind because I'd be working for him now. Then he pulled out some clothes from the wardrobe and said we'd have a bit of fancy dress and wouldn't I look great in the

8

schoolgirl's outfit with the white socks and plaits in my
hair.

'Try it on,' he said, 'then come in and give us a show.
I'll have a little present for you after, but only if you cheer
up.' He pointed to a stash of polythene packets in a box on
the mahogany dresser.

When he'd gone and shut the door behind him I stood
looking around at all the mirrors; it was like the room was
full of people in black tracksuits, all of them with orange
hair and the face of a born idiot. I was thinking you could
have snuffed me out like a candle and all those in the
mirror would still be there, miserable as sin. Thinking of
candles got me remembering the one me and Maeve had
lit for our mother in front of the statue of the Blessed
Virgin, and Maeve saying I could pay for the damn thing
with my own pennies because hadn't I been the favourite
and hadn't she been landed in the shite with me to look
out for and our father being the old bugger that he was,
and I'd her to thank that I'd never been his favourite and
if I didn't know what she meant by that then I was deaf
and blind as well as stupid, like our mother must have
been, and if I wasn't as green as I was cabbage-looking
then I was to keep my bloody mouth shut anyway, God
knows she'd enough practice at shutting hers. She's been
a good sister to me all these years.

I'd just got the tracksuit off me when I heard him in the
front room shouting at me to hurry up. I left the school
uniform he put out for me and thought I'd take a quick
look inside the wardrobe. It was full of the kind of frocks
that Maeve would have called tarty, some of them with a
big gap at the front so you'd be hanging out at the top
with everything showing. There were frocks made of rub-
bery stuff and PVC with metal studs and boots to match,
whips too, hanging over the rail. Right at the end was

something long and black and soft. A nun's habit it was, with everything just right – headdress, scapular and all, even rosary beads hanging out from the side pocket. It was like a birthday present got specially for me. I put it on and looked in the mirrors.

'Lady,' I said, 'I'm ready for you now,' and I knew in my heart she was listening and nearer to me than the skin on my body.

I left the seventy-five pence on the mahogany dresser, as I'd be having no use for earthly riches any more, but I took a good wad of the polythene packets with the white powder and stuffed them into my pocket. I'm greener than cabbage-looking but I'm not stupid.

I went across the passage hoping to let myself out with no one hearing, but he heard me and said, 'You took your bloody time,' so I nipped into the toilet and bolted the door, thinking I'd maybe pretend to have the runs and then he'd get bored and forget about me or go to sleep or something.

He came and stood outside, drumming his fingers on the door. 'Hurry up, you, whatever your name is.'

I said, 'Marie, and I think I've got the runs,' and he said, 'What?' so I said it again and Jerry's brother said, 'I know that voice – what's her name?' and the other one said, 'Marie,' and next they were both stood in the passage with Jerry saying about how he was going to carve me up good so no one would touch me with a barge pole after he'd finished and the other one saying he could carve what he liked of his own property but I was his and finders keepers.

While they were bickering on I was saying three Hail Marys for a small miracle and thinking that it would be a fine thing now for her to come and wallop the bejazus out of the two of them.

'Tell you what,' said the one, 'let's toss for it.'

Jerry's brother sounded a bit grumpy but he said, 'Yeah, all right, got any change?'

'No,' said the other, 'I only got notes.'

I shouted that there was some change on the dresser in the bedroom and he went off to get it while Jerry's brother went back to the front room and turned the telly up to get the football results. I nipped out of the toilet, quiet as a fly on the wall, and out the front door with no one seeing me at all, not bothering to close it in case they heard the click of it shutting. I made for the stairs, nearly tripping over the habit which was maybe a fraction too long for me.

I'd just got into Euston Road when a heel from one of my shoes began to wobble about, so I took them off and threw them to the side. They'd not been very comfortable anyway, though Maeve had said they would do for the wedding, and the white satin was all torn and dirty with me being run off my feet all day.

A policeman saw me and said, 'Are you all right, Sister?' and I said yes and saw Jerry's brother and the other one coming up behind me so I talked on a bit about the hot weather we'd been having and the mercy it was to have a bit of rain.

'It's stopped raining now, Sister,' said the policeman and I said, 'Thanks be to God,' and the two men passed by as though I'd been invisible. They were looking for a girl in school uniform with bright red hair, not a bride of Christ. There's something to be said for not standing out in a crowd, though it would maybe look a bit strange with the black make-up and rouge still on my face.

I was nearing Kings Cross when I spotted a girl I recognized standing on the corner of Argyll Street, still in the wet clothes and sniffing. I asked her if she was wanting something and she said, 'Sister, you can't give me what I want,' so then I pulled out a wad of the polythene packets and handed them over, and her eyes opened up wide and swivelled about as she opened one of them and tasted a bit with her little finger the way Jerry's brother had done.

She whispered, 'Jesus! God bless you, Sister,' and I went off hoping to find the other one, which I did, outside the Burger Delight as before, only it was all closed up, it being near midnight.

She was stood there in her mini-skirt and black stilettos and I said, 'God bless you,' and stood next to her for a few minutes, saying nothing, watching the cars slow down, and the men in them giving her the eye then speeding up again when they caught sight of me; and she said, 'Give us a break, will you, Sister?'

So then I handed over the rest of the polythene packets and walked off without waiting to hear what she'd say, thinking that a good turn doesn't need any thanks.

I'm here now. I'm standing underneath the lamplight. I thought I saw her by the station, but it was only a woman in a blue raincoat, waiting for a taxi. She will come for me any minute now.

The streets are emptier than before, the cars creeping by in slow motion. I can see other people waiting – girls of about my age, and older, and younger. The woman in the black stilettos is staring at me.

The bells are starting to chime out the count of twelve and I'm praying with my eyes shut, Lady, because prayer is like faith, you can move mountains with it and walk across water, it's white magic, pure as snow, Lady, under the blue, and what would it be but faith itself keeps the world spinning round and all the planets moving in the darkness, worlds without end?

Oh, Lady, full of grace, come for me now, blessed among women, don't throw me off into the night with nothing at all, come, Lady, come now.

Ramping on Her Shield

Christina Dunhill

I am the lion. A huntress. I run after deer. I must have what is dear to me, will make it dear to me, holding it between my forepaws and licking it. I'll protect you, I mumble, between nuzzles, will give you love and make you precious, lick you new as a cub.

I would like to be clever but am not. I like to snooze in the afternoon sun, lying along the branch of a tree with an ear to the birds. I can be made happy. If you stroke the back of my neck or fondle my ears I'll yawn so wide you could put your head in my mouth.

Friends indulge me. They tell me stories and, from time to time, do not neglect to whisper I'm the boss, the queen-lady. One is easily deceived.

I sleep a lot. It's the charge of the too-lately live flesh in my body. I eat meat. Jump the running hind and sink my teeth into its neck, feel its body fold under me as its legs buckle and the breath goes out of it.

The only animal I have felt the breath go out of was Thumper, my ginger cat, my alter ego, my playmate. He died from a playing accident; fell off the bathroom window sill as I was teasing him. The vet rang after two days; I heard his voice behind hers, wailing. When I arrived, he

lay on his side in a hutch, in the racks of hutches, shriek-
ing, his arm rising and falling. 'Oh Thumper, I love you
so much. My darling boy, you've meant the world to me.'
He stopped wailing as soon as I started and lay still. He
couldn't understand. 'He knows your voice,' said the vet,
embarrassed, 'he's listening to you.'

He couldn't understand. This is about death. The long
and rigid night. He screamed then, louder than ever, and
lifted his arm again. How could I consign him to death?
How could I live with that? 'Oh, baby,' I said, 'it's going
to be over.' He stopped crying when the needle went in his
arm. Then his sides stopped moving. He went slack in my
hands.

He was in agony, the way he used to have pleasure. He
was all agony. The way he used to have a wank or groom
his sister, the way he used to play. I remember him in
sudden passion for a friend of mine, lying diagonally with
his haunches in her lap and his head on her breasts, gazing
into her eyes and dribbling. I picture him ascending the
airy firmament to a waiting Virgin. She is hunkered down
with her blue robe pulled up on her knees, making cluck-
ing noises. Thumper trots up like a cat in second kitten-
hood, like he always was, but in the flesh too he is a young
cat again now, smaller, redder and unarthritic.

'Come on, baby boy,' she says. He lets the Virgin pick
him up and clasp him to her bosom. Rattle, rattle, he goes,
purring and nosing her neck and blinking into her eyes.

At night all things turn into what they are not. The cats
went out and I lay with my girlfriend. In the beginning
was the word. I couldn't take my mouth off her; the taste
went round my palate like cannabis and I thought I'd
never be hungry again. I was the mother who coos at her
baby, who smooths the bedding and jiggles the coloured

balls on the string to hear her infant gurgle. She kicks her plump legs and waves her arms to be lifted. I pick her up in her summer blanket and kiss her under her little milky ear.

My girlfriend sings country, Mexico County south american pop. Her voice comes twanging out like a cat's, dangling all winsome round the vowel sounds, arcing way up but hanging back in with the low and knowing. We made love in her trailer, drinking strong black tea brewed in a kettle. I'd kiss her through the holes in her T-shirt, get so high I'd hardly sleep for nights in a row. 'Sing for me?' I'd say sometimes. You never heard anything like that girl sing when she's choked up.

'Not now,' she'd moan, 'when we're out driving.' And she'd drop into sleep heavy as a schoolboy, but alert as an alley cat, while I'd drift with my face in her blond tobacco hair, sniffing it high up into memory.

She told me stories of travelling, travelling, travelling, away from her dad's anger, but it was with us all the time, right in the middle of us, in the butter seeping into the hot toast and the way she never sat still, never seemed to finish more than two sentences, never came, and always walked out when we were getting anywhere. I'd take her fingers and scoop the nails clean with mine, then suck the rest of the dirt off till they'd go whorled and creased like a baby's in a bath. She'd cry then sometimes.

'It's all right, we're safe here.'

'I want to be invisible.'

'I know.'

'Everywhere I go it comes back and grounds me. I can't get away. It's in everything I want most, things just turn inside out when I get near them.'

'I know. Trust me. I love you.'

17

'It's not a matter of loving me, you klutz. Do you think my dad didn't love me?'

That's how it went. I had a good idea of what she was talking about. I'd noticed how she always tried to be drunk if she knew we were going to do it. I'd feel her body go into tension, turn into sprung coils of muscle ready to repulse me as soon as she got to feel anything, almost as if the feelings themselves turned traitor on her, those tiny feelings that come swimming up so pretty and guileless, like fish in an aquarium; they were torpedoes to her, she'd scupper them. She'd get up and open the door, sit on the step rolling cigarettes, with the bottle of Jack Daniels beside her. And she'd go hard then and I'd want to hit her.

My little cat would laugh. I remember the first time he saw a friend of mine in her fancy Norwegian slipper-socks, he couldn't get his mouth closed. You know, the fancy knitted things that start below the knee in socks and end in little suede soles. He climbed on a chair and fell to sucking the spaces between his claws. She forgot all about him, walked past his chair. Dead hit. The spring, the deadly nip, the smother. That slipper never spoke another word.

I made friends with a hairdresser for a little while. She was over from LA on training. She cut my hair in a wedge, a dream cut that gave me a sleek black curtain over one eye which swung all around and hung right back in place if you shook your head. Like your first pleated skirt. I couldn't see out of one eye, but that was fine. She only came to my place once. I met her at the bus stop. She got so tired walking up the hill, she had to rest. 'Listen,' she said, 'is this the slums?'

She sat on the sofa asking me whether it was more important to travel – the firm had salons in Paris and

18

Rome – or to go back to her boyfriend before he took up with someone else. She held her cup in one hand and the saucer in the other. Thumper sat on her lap trying to win her attention. He and I were both thinking how well his fur went with her red hair. She and I were both hoping not too much of it would come off on her black silk suit. She shivered slightly and I pushed the paraffin heater nearer her. Thumper turned to the heat and smacked her hand playfully, sending the smooth Jamaican coffee over her smoother designer trousers. I rushed for a damp cloth. 'Sure,' she said gratefully, and, after a pause, 'I wonder what he's doing now.'

A month or so later she sent a care package. I knew what it was because that's what the note said: 'Hope you like the care package.' It was an enormous blue fleecy babygro with feet and a hood. I thought of a big blue snowman. That winter I slept in my babygro and never took it off if I didn't have to go out. Thumper admired it. It was the first time he'd taken to pouncing on me from a height – a dangerous initiative for us both. Thumper was not a slight cat. Luckily, he spent most of his time dozing in the oven. If I was sitting in the kitchen with friends, I'd have the oven on with the door down and he'd lie on it. He loved a nice gas fire.

This is for you, Thumper, thirteen years of my life. Remember how we used to lie together in the hallway when the carpet had just been laid, all thick and heavenly under the nose? How you lay on your side and pulled yourself along the whole length of it with your front claws, checking over your shoulder to see when I'd go for you but I didn't have the heart and you rolled round and round and stretched your spine out backwards like a boomerang to make me put my face in your tight little belly so you could capture my hair?

I wanted to be the best for my girlfriend, to go ramping on her shield. Put me on your notepaper, I'd say. Put me on your breast pocket.

'I want to go home,' she said.

'Why?'

'I can feel something.'

'How do you mean?'

'Something calling me.'

'Probably your sister. "Come back, Kerry, you bastard, do your share."'

'Maybe. I'm going home.'

'You've got no money.'

'I've got my airfare.'

I had a flash of anger: all the times she'd bummed money off me.

'Look, this isn't going anywhere.'

I think my mouth fell open.

'I can't carry anyone. I don't need you here. You think you've got to cheer me up. Listen, I don't want to be saved. I want to stop *caring*.'

'Is it because . . . ?'

'My agent's got me a tour.'

I smiled at the thought of her all cute in the big skirt and the blouse with puff sleeves; then I remembered the beer-swilling truck drivers, the farmers, her dad, and wanted to throw up. Singing country, the good old humdingin' down home values.

'I'll have to leave in just over a week.'

'I see.'

When we return to the children we rub cheeks all the way down their flanks. We share the kill, the sisters and I, and we share the eating of it, just as we have shared the suckling. We teach the children the pride and the knowl-

20

edge; this is for sovereignty; we teach them the respect
which is survival. Respect all that moves but cannot be
eaten. Respect, in particular, the Elephant. Elephant sisters and brothers work for the Great Spirit. It has been
given to them to know the rituals. It is because they live
three lifetimes and are so long in the womb. Theirs is the
decorum and the mysteries have been explained to them.
We tell the young ones the stories.

> *Elephant pulled down a big tree and was still rooting in*
> *its branches when a person came crashing by, and, find-*
> *ing the tree blocking its path, clambered over it, quite*
> *unaware. Elephant emerged, angered, trumpeting.*
> *Person tried to hide. Elephant trunked it out from under*
> *the foliage and pounded it underfoot until it was gone.*
> *And all the forest floor in that clearing was churned to*
> *dust and not one sign of the person that was. Every*
> *afternoon for a month Elephant returned to the clearing*
> *and stood there till evening, ears flapping and trunk to*
> *the sky.*

I carried my dead cat round the garden at the end of the
day. In his box. Lifted him to the heavens, howling: 'What
d'you call this, then? What *is* this?'

He used to love boxes. They made him feel like a knight
in a castle, like a victor. If you walked by, he'd flash out
and lay siege to your ankle. I saw him trying a variation
of this game on bushes in the garden when I'd left a plant
box outside.

'It'll have to be before morning,' said my friends. 'In the
morning he'll be stiff as a stone.' I couldn't do it. Fur and
earth don't go. Couldn't do it till the sun went down.

I left Kerry the following morning and didn't go back for

a couple of days. Nothing hurts like your love thrown back at you, like knowing you've made no difference.

I wanted to talk but she wouldn't. I said I'd call round at the weekend and pick up my stuff. When I did she wasn't there. The trailer looked tidy, as if she'd already done her packing. I guessed she'd taken a last opportunity to buy her folks some Marks and Spencer jumpers. I went to the toilet before I left. There was a bit of a queue; only two of the three cubicles seemed to be working. When they'd gone in ahead of me I kicked open the other door, and pulled it off when it fell on top of her.

'You're so boring,' I shouted. 'Couldn't you surprise me?' I started to slap her.

She grinned at me, head lolling to one side, then threw up. 'Leave me alone.'

'You stupid bloody brainless little git.' I pulled her upright by the collar. I don't know what I had in mind but the women were out by then. They tore me away from her.

'Bloody animals!' said one.

'Just get her to hospital, you hear!' I shouted and ran back to the trailer. I collected my things and left.

It is a sadness. I am sadder than a hungry jackal without her pack. There's a spot where, sucking at a graze from a rhino's horn, I've chewed a patch of fur off my flank. I try to doze the sun out with my sisters but the branch irritates my belly. My dreams are loud with the colours of feathers, and birdsong, things that belong to the heavens. It's getting harder to hold the shapes on the horizon line fast against the heat haze. I suppose my eyes are failing.

22

A Good Mother

Wendy Wallace

The baby sat propped against a cushion in the corner of the couch. His eyes were bloodshot and his head drooped forwards, his chin resting on his chest. He looked morose and elderly. Jane crouched on the carpet, holding his feet in her hands and kissing them through the thin towelling of his stretch suit. She already knew what she was going to call him.

The wail of a passing police siren bounced off the glass of the window and the baby began to cry. Jane bent over him. 'Don't,' she said, lifting him awkwardly to her shoulder. 'Please don't cry.' She straightened and started to pace the room, hugging him to her. Her heart was pounding. She pulled his cardigan down over his rounded back and took a deep breath. 'Hush little baby, don't say a word.' She cleared her throat and started again in a lower pitch. 'Mama's gonna buy you a mockingbird.'

It was getting dark outside. It was that time of day when other people hurried purposefully to well-lit homes and she sat, often, in the near darkness, unable to turn off the dripping tap or turn on the heating, unable to find cheer within or without.

She walked and sang, rubbing her nose over the baby's head. A faint smell of someone else's perfume clung to his

23

downy hair. Had her mother paced the floor like this? she
wondered, as she moved mechanically to and fro. Unlikely.
Her mother couldn't bear babies. Or so she had been fond
of saying, at coffee mornings and to babysitters. 'One was
enough for me,' she would say, laughing. 'More than
enough.'

The baby had stopped crying. She lowered him gingerly
onto the couch. She sat down cautiously next to him and
lit a cigarette, waving the smoke away from him with her
free hand. 'My mother nearly died when I was born,' she
said, glancing at the baby. That was something else she
had heard from behind the armchair, sitting in a secret
corner by the bookshelf, where the sitting-room carpet was
untrodden, the pile still thick and the colour chrysan-
themum bright. That was where she learnt about her
mother's delicate foot lashing out at the midwife with the
strength of a horse, and heard how her throat had been
sore for days afterwards from the screaming.

The baby started hiccoughing. 'Are you hungry darling?'
she whispered. She went into the kitchen and took a feed-
ing bottle and an unopened tin of dried milk out of the
drawer by the sink. She filled the kettle and measured
four scoopfuls of powder into the bottle, carefully levelling
off the top of the scoop with a knife. She put the bottle to
cool in a bowl of cold water and carried it into the living
room.

The baby looked at her without curiosity and grimaced.
His nails were blue and a line of dark fur covered the rim
of his ears. His hands sketched the air, surprised to meet
no resistance. Jane sat down and closed her eyes. She was
back in her parents' house, lying in her bed in the darkness, listening. Laughter and the smell of meat cooking in
wine drifted in waves up the stairs. Then her mother's
voice met her ears, a drinks-fuelled, in-company voice, not

the low sound of her at-home one. She was still awake at midnight, when her mother came in, preoccupied and perfumed, to kiss her goodnight. Her mother was wearing her scarlet dress.

She was in her mother's bedroom, watching her pull the scarlet dress out of the wardrobe. It was Thai silk, tailored, with darts at the bust and the waist. She was sitting on the slippery eiderdown of her parents' bed, fiddling with the drawer of the bedside cabinet where her mother kept her Dutch cap and her Mary McCarthy novels, her Pond's cold cream and her wedding ring which she always took off when she went to bed. Jane wondered if she was still married when she was asleep.

She laid the baby on his back and undid the press studs on his babygro. She took off the nappy and smiled with satisfaction. His testicles were purple and over-sized. She wiped them with a cotton-wool ball and rolled his penis between her fingers.

MaryAnne, her doll had been called. Not her best doll but her biggest one. MaryAnne had eyes of blue and an unflinching smile. She wasn't a doll you could love, only dress and undress. Rose was her best doll. Rose was a plastic baby with rounded limbs and curled fingers. Jane had never had a boy dolly with a little moulded penis between his legs. They didn't make them then. You knew they were girls by their yellow hair, by the rosebuds on their dresses. There was nothing between their legs but smooth innocent plastic. It had shocked her when Rose's leg had fallen off, revealing her dark, hollow insides with black rubber guts holding on her head and her other limbs. She had wondered if everybody was like that inside. She doubted it. She would be full of corned beef and Angel Delight. Mrs Campbell had a baby in her tummy.

Jane shook a few drops of the milk onto the back of her

hand. It was still too hot. She picked up the baby and held him in the crook of her arm, lifting her sweater and freeing one breast from her bra. As she pointed it towards him he darted at the nipple, open-mouthed, like a baby bird. After some false starts his mouth closed around her and he began sucking with all his might.

She had never been breastfed. Her mother would have been horrified by the idea. Would have blushed to think of the milk leaking out through the scarlet evening dress in two shaming patches. She had been afraid it would spoil her figure. By that she meant that she feared that her breasts would hang low like some African woman in a TV documetary. So she opted for Cow and Gate, four-hourly. You were safe with Cow and Gate; Cow and Gate and Playtex.

The baby clenched her nipple between iron gums and Jane squeaked with pain. Then he pushed it out of his mouth and began screaming in earnest, his face grown suddenly ugly. She pulled her sweater down guiltily, and pushed the rubber teat into his mouth. She knew, really, that she wouldn't be able to feed him. But it might come. She had read about it, about women lactating through love; love and sucking. Grandmothers, even, had got milk in their breasts. She held him tight and gazed at him as he sucked on the bottle, a dribble of milk running down from the corner of his mouth and disappearing into a roll of fat under his chin. His free hand waved in the air, as if he were signalling to someone. He drained the bottle and continued to suck on the empty teat.

She wondered if he wanted more. Four ounces at each feed, for a newborn, but that was just an average. She laid him on his stomach across her knees and rubbed his back. He belched, and a spurt of white milk dropped onto the carpet. At least he wouldn't starve.

26

She had begun by buying things for a layette. A layette was what you had before you had a baby. Anyone might prepare a layette. She would have one instead of a baby. She would love the miniature socks, the vests tied at the front with narrow satin ribbons, the broderie anglaise quilts and velvety bathtowels; it was easy enough to do so. She began collecting things from Mothercare, just as she had once collected outfits for Sindy. Sindy's riding clothes, with the black boots and tiny whip, Sindy's ice-skating costume, with the mauve tutu and white rabbit's fur muff. Sindy had an outfit for every occasion. And so, after a while, did her baby. Everything in blue or yellow, because her baby was going to be a boy.

She had begged her mother for a brother. Even a sister would have done. But her mother had insisted. 'You're enough for me, darling.' And when Jane pressed the point her voice would grow sharp and high. 'I'm not having another bloody baby, darling. Not for anyone.'

With the baby still over her knees, she noticed a small red birthmark on the back of his head, between his fine dark hair and the neck of his babygro. She peered at it, feeling it with her fingers. It disturbed her. It meant he could always be recognized. Even when he was old, when his hair had come and gone, and his eyes grown sad, he could be known by his blemish. She turned the baby over, trying to put the thought out of her mind.

For a long time she had just pretended. Laying a place for her imaginary brother at mealtimes, saving half her sweets for him, telling the girls at school about him. And then there had been Jack. And she had chosen him. She had watched his house from her bedroom window until one Tuesday morning Mrs Campbell had gone out to the shop in her slippers. Then she had let herself in through the garden door, run up the stairs, and lifted the baby out

27

of his carrycot. She had left MaryAnne for Mrs Campbell as a sort of consolation. She hadn't intended to, but the cot looked so sad and empty without Jack she had felt sorry for Mrs Campbell. She knew what it was like to have an empty cot. She had had one at home for days, all ready for Jack. It was only a wooden box, but lined with her best nightdress and with a small cushion off the couch for a pillow it looked just like a baby's bed.

She had crept down the stairs, holding the baby tightly round the middle, and run back to her own house. She had made him comfortable in the box, popped a Love Heart in his mouth, hidden him under her bed and gone to school.

Mrs Campbell had never recovered from finding the blue-eyed MaryAnne in brown-eyed Jack's bed. Jane had never forgiven her mother for giving him back. Of course she could understand it now. How could a baby live in a box under a bed? And she hadn't had any of the things a baby needed then. Now she had everything. She had the Moses basket and the baby bath, gripe water and a listening plug, a lamb's skin to comfort him and a months' supply of nappies. And most of all she had love. Enough for a lifetime, love which would never grow old or get dirty or be handed down. Yes, she would make a good mother.

She looked at her watch. Seven o'clock. She felt exultant. The baby depended on her and she had not failed him. He was warm and fed and alive. It seemed a miracle. But as she sat watching him sleep the pleasure faded.

She gave a small shudder. Now she had Jack, she would have to be cheerful. She could not be lonely, for his sake. She would wind up a music box and put on the washing machine, fill the house with the smell of baby powder and onions frying in olive oil, she would affirm that there were lives being lived within these walls. She would run a bath, chop vegetables, sing. The telephone would ring, and the doorbell, and she would answer, without dread. She would not hear the clock ticking or the tap dripping; they would be drowned out by the gurgling of the baby, the chink of glasses. The jars and bottles in the kitchen would not fix her with glassy stares, the packets and boxes would stop their whispering, the saved yogurt pots would be given meaning by his presence. The wind would not dare to rattle the windows of a house so convincingly inhabited.

When he was bigger he could tear pages out of her glossiest books and break her best cups, he could draw on the walls and scoop earth out of plant pots with strong, fat fingers. He could pee on the carpet and climb on the couch with his shoes on and she would be glad.

But for now he slept, his spirit wandering out of the house and beyond her reach, and she was more alone than ever. She put her ear to his mouth. She could hear nothing. Then she noticed the slight rise and fall of his cardigan. She sat up, relieved. There seemed to be nothing to do but wait for him to wake up.

Our Sweetness and Our Hope

Frances Gapper

The ocean at night swallows up every light. Even the
moon's beams are sucked in. The water is dead cold. I am
going into it very slowly, feet first, letting it creep up me,
a prolonged unbearable shudder. The waves nibble at me
like tiny fish.

I have a terrible deep wound in me somewhere. Go into
the sea, she said, let the salt water heal you. I'm swimming
now, carrying myself swiftly out in the darkness. Hanging
on the surface, depths unfolding below me, where huge
things move silently. They smell my blood, though I'm not
bleeding. Sharks. Big mouths full of teeth, razor-sharp,
white, lethal. They could shear off an arm or a leg so
casually it would feel just like a passing bump, a nudge.
Or half my body gone. Just like that.

A joke. I hate practical jokes. I'd rather see it coming to
me, glimpse the teeth before I'm inside the shark. Which
parts of me will it spit out again, which parts savour as
delicacies?

Nothing breaks surface or betrays itself by so much as
a ripple. Darkness and utter silence. I put my face down
in the water, open my eyes forcibly and look. The light
instantly dazzles me, glorious underwater golden-green

31

light. The sharks – three sharks, four – are drifting contentedly in the golden depths.

Then the light goes off. I'm jolted awake. We've reached the terminus, the bus garage. I've travelled by night bus all the way from Trafalgar Square. The impatient bus driver is flicking his lights on and off, to encourage my departure. I put my book away – it is *Jaws*, the original paperback by Peter Benchley. A young woman flitters up from the back seat, like a startled moth. She looks exceedingly pale, bloodless, drained. Perhaps it's just the light.

This was my first meeting with Selina. The dream introduced her to me, contained and presented in neat metaphor all the most important elements of our future relationship: blood, danger, a hidden enemy, unexpected reversals of light and darkness, fear and attraction – all suggested themselves, without a word spoken.

Song of the Vampire (*anon – a translation*)
I am too full of blood tonight
The moon's white face is masked in a veil of blood
Blood drips from her, like tears
I am flesh made by the moon, my lady mother and cruel
  mistress . . .

Selina explained vaguely that she came from 'outside London'. Her voice was curiously lacking in timbre, but with a harsh, grating accent. Of course it never occurred to me that she was a vampire. Otherwise I might have thought twice about inviting her back to my flat.

She was remarkably colourless; not so much pale as emptied of colour, bleached dry, like bone. She conveyed the effect of a negative photograph, something one stage removed from real. She was like a vacuum, everything disappeared into her. Words, thoughts. I chattered inanely as we walked along the pavement, she smiled and said nothing. I wondered why I was putting myself out so, for a stranger. But she had this attractive quality – of being fictional, obviously not true, a character from a story or legend.

And since I have already let slip that she was a vampire, you may be curious to know what happened between us. Whether she bit me and whether – since yes, she did, and obviously I survived the experience – she then allowed me the opportunity of biting her, and if so, whether I proceeded with due caution, keeping in mind (a) the peril of my immortal soul and (b) the HIV virus and the danger of its transference through exchange of blood, not to speak of Hepatitis B.

Not until many moons later did Selina draw blood from me, and then only with the greatest reluctance. The reason for her translucent paleness, on our first meeting, was that she had given up vampirism. She had gone to the opposite extreme, or perhaps not, of becoming a Roman Catholic. She wore a cross around her neck. She thought it would protect her, from other vampires perhaps, or from herself.

She confided shyly in me that she was taking instruction at the Roman Catholic church of St Mary the Virgin at Southgate. Now I have an utter and complete horror of Catholicism, having myself, like a remarkable number of other lesbians, been brought up in the faith. I am still not free of that legacy of years. 'Catholics!' I exclaimed, with an indrawn hiss. 'I should steer well clear of them, if I were you. Unless you enjoy sadomasochism in the name of love.'

We stood together under the orange streetlamp, below my flat. I wondered, should I invite her up for coffee? Her eyes were silver-grey, enormous in the strange light.

'It's my family,' she said simply. 'The problem is my family.'

'Oh?'

'My mother in particular. She doesn't like me associating with common mortals. What she calls "mixing it".'

'Who else are you supposed to associate with? Immortals?' I laughed.

'Immortals, yes.'

'Your mother sounds a bit odd.'

'She is – ' Selina hesitated. 'She only drinks every couple of years. But then she really goes for it.'

'On a pub crawl?'

'A trail of bloodless corpses.'

I presumed bloodless corpses was slang for empty glasses or bottles. So the old lady was an alcoholic. 'But your mother isn't here now.'

Selina glanced round nervously. Something fluttered beyond the circle of light – a bat or a moth. 'She still snoops on me. Excuse me.' Selina turned. 'Fuck off, fuck off!' she screeched into the darkness.

I saw something run like a huge spider, graceful and swift, straight up the smooth vertical sidewall of my neighbour's house. 'Excuse me,' Selina said again. 'We had better go indoors. I think I will, after all, take up your kind offer of a bed for the night.'

I could not recall having made any such kind offer. But I was too tired to argue.

I made Selina up a bed in the sitting room. She was asleep when I left for work next morning. And when I came back from work, there she was, still fast asleep.

Her silver-ash hair spread around her, falling over the pillows to the floor. It looked as though she was lying in a pool of metal. Maybe that would account, I thought, for the pallor of her skin, her air of exhaustion. The hair was draining all her strength.

34

It is my evening custom to smoke a cigarette on the balcony outside my bedroom window. The balcony is about two yards by one yard, enough to accommodate one deck-chair and one potted plant. It is 'structurally unsound', as the surveyor informed me when I moved into the flat ten years ago; also the floor is rotten and likely to collapse at any moment, in which case I should plunge to a certain death. This adds a pleasant spice of danger to my evening ritual. I smoke Silk Cut, having been seduced by the sub-liminally violent advertisements e.g. the chainsaw wrapped up in purple silk.

The sun slipped behind the industrial estate. I was just stubbing out my cigarette when Selina appeared. She wore an old-fashioned black dress, high necked, with long, tight sleeves ending in black frills at the wrists. 'That's an addiction,' she said, pointing at the ashtray in my lap.

'It's an addiction I happen to enjoy.'

'You'll taste horrible.'

'Smoking has certainly affected my sense of taste – I suppose it's the' – my voice faltered – 'er, sorry, what did you just say?'

Selina leant against the window frame, looking pale and elegant. I noticed she had very long, white fingers and toes. Her bare feet seemed extraordinarily narrow. I wondered fleetingly how she ever got shoes to fit them. 'Where I come from, people are judged like wines, in terms of their purity and "body". A strong taint of tobacco can be ruinous. I don't think you'd appeal to connoisseurs like my sister Ludmilla, for instance, but then Ludmilla has an excep-tionally discriminating palate. She can scarcely drink any-thing stronger than the fresh blood of a tender newborn babe . . . it's very difficult for her. Newborn babes are so well guarded nowadays, even against common baby snat-chers, let alone vampires. It was different a couple of centuries back, when baby girls would frequently be exposed and left to die on the hillsides – then Ludmilla had a wonderful time.'

'I expect she did. So your sister is a vampire?' I coughed over the word.

'Yes. We all are, all seven of us.'

'Good heavens.'

'But I'm trying to change.' Selina anxiously twisted her long fingers together. 'It limits one's social life dreadfully. You're just starting to get to know someone interesting, then it's so tempting to bite them, and then of course they die – or become vampires. So boring. I want to broaden my horizons. I think it's happening already. I'm really beginning to *appreciate* people – not just how they taste, but for themselves.'

'If you want to broaden your horizons, I would forget about Catholicism.'

'Oh, but the priest – he's so nice. Father Michael. He helped me to stop drinking.'

I remembered the bloodless corpses. 'Don't you, er, drink at all nowadays?'

'Strawberry milkshake,' Selina said solemnly. 'Nothing else.'

'My dear girl. Does it provide you with the right nutrients?'

'No, but it's good for my soul.'

'How charming,' I said, with a touch of condescension, thinking how sweet and naive she was. Those godawful Catholics. 'I didn't think vampires had souls.'

Selina turned even paler than before, literally white at the lips. Her fingernails, I noticed, were clear as glass. 'By God's grace,' she said, 'I'll receive one tomorrow, when I'm baptized.'

36

The next day was Sunday and Selina's baptism was scheduled for three o'clock. I drove her to the church, feeling it was the least I could do in the circumstances – she was by now in a state of teeth-chattering terror. There was hardly any traffic, until we stopped at some lights; then I glimpsed a big black car, like a hearse, pulling out of a side road. I glanced in the driving mirror. There was the car, behind us, but it seemed to be empty. I remarked on this to Selina, who glanced over her shoulder. 'Oh my God!' she shrieked. 'It's my family! Drive on, drive on!'

I could not resist looking round, which was a bad mistake. The hearse, I could now see, contained seven women dressed in black. Selina's mother sat in the front passenger seat, distinguished by her thin, aristocratic nose and glittering eyes. The chauffeur, underneath his peaked cap, was obviously dead, and rapidly decomposing.

The lights changed and I slammed my foot down on the accelerator – luckily I knew an alternative route, and we arrived at the church on time.

Agremina

Selina told me this story, of her love affair with a mortal woman:

I've sucked blood from countless numbers of women. Some died, some survived. But I've only been in love once. Her name was Agremina and she lived in the nineteenth century, in rural Transylvania. I met her outside the town alehouse, late one night – she was waiting for her father, who often needed help getting home. I was just waiting – you know – for anyone who might come stumbling out of the alehouse door. Drunkards are easy prey, even if they taste foul. We got talking, and I told her I was a vampire.

37

She wasn't afraid. We talked about – oh, all kinds of things. Especially books. We had the same tastes in literature, it turned out; she liked Emily Dickinson too. And we both loved walking in the mountains.

It felt as if we'd known each other all our lives. She was so beautiful and so good, I fell in love with her at first sight. And she felt the same way about me. She told me so. 'You don't mind me being a vampire, then?' I said anxiously.

'Oh Selina, I don't think of you as a vampire.'

Well in the early days that was enough, she made me happy, and the kissing and so on was lovely, but then increasingly I began to feel terribly frustrated. The wanting to bite feeling – it became awfully strong.

So I wrote her a letter, a farewell letter, saying it was best we should part, although I still loved her desperately. After I'd sent the letter I heard nothing from her for a week or more. I stayed in the castle, pacing up and down my room, in agony and torment. One night, when the moon was full, I went up on the castle battlements, and through the trees I glimpsed my mother's carriage – that was before she got a car – bowling at a fast pace down the long winding road to the town.

Instantly I was seized with a dread suspicion. Throwing my cloak around me, I sped downstairs to the shed where I kept my rusty old black bicycle, and was soon in desperate pursuit. But it was too late. When I reached the town my mother's carriage was nowhere to be seen. I went straight to Agremina's house. It was plunged in darkness. I climbed through her bedroom window and managed to light a candle. She was lying on the bed, deathly pale. She only just had enough strength left to gasp a few words. She had written a letter, saying that she loved me, that she would give me – everything, that she would be waiting for me

38

that night. My mother had intercepted the letter and –
you can guess the rest.

I slashed my wrist and held it to Agremina's lips. I
begged her on my knees to drink – to drink my own heart's
blood, to live forever – but she was too weak by then. She
turned her face away from me, and died.

Now can you wonder that I hold my mother in such
hatred?

While Selina was being baptized, I sat chainsmoking in
the car outside. Not long after our arrival I saw the hearse
slide up the road like a crocodile and park by the cemetery
gates. Selina's sisters emerged and clambered over the
wall, with the ungainly groping movements of night creatures in sunlight. Her mother and the deceased chauffeur
remained inside the car. Although she never once looked
in my direction, I'm sure she knew I was there.

Through the cemetery gates I could see Selina's sisters
dancing around the gravestones, their black garments
flapping. The clock on the church tower showed 3.15, and
as its two hands joined to a single pointing arrow, I heard
a terrible unearthly scream from the church. The sisters
went into a huddle – incidentally, a huddle is the collective
noun for vampires. I was immediately convinced that
Selina was being tortured or even murdered inside the
church; indeed baptism has always seemed to me a terrible
act of violence, pouring cold water over a screaming innocent child, wrenching the devil out of her. And with a poor
vampire, presumably forcing the 'soul' in. Any spare 'soul'
the priest happens to have lying around in the vestry,
inside some dusty cupboard?

I wrenched open the car door and hurried up the path
towards the church. Selina's sisters came leaping and

bounding over the graves towards me, waving their arms, but just in time I slipped inside the porch.

Not pausing to read the notices about cleaning rotas and harvest festivals, I cautiously lifted the heavy iron latch and entered the darkened church. Furious whisperings could be heard up by the font; stealing behind a pillar, I saw a hatted woman of respectable appearance, proffering a first aid kit. The priest was fumbling with a tube of Savlon. Selina was looking terrified and guilty, with wet hair. I beckoned frantically at her and she hurried towards me, trembling.

'I bit him,' she whispered.

'You bit the priest?'

'When he poured the holy water on me – it scalded my skin like fire. I couldn't help – it wasn't really a bite. I just sort of grazed him.'

'Oh dear, Selina.'

'You're a very ungrateful young lady!' exclaimed the hatted woman in scandalized tones. 'Look what you've done to poor Father Michael. You'll need a tetanus injection for that, Father.' And she urged him solicitously away into the vestry.

'Let's go,' Selina said, on the verge of tears.

'Your sisters have got the church surrounded.'

'I'll fight my way out.'

'You're not strong enough, dear. They've fed well recently, from the look of them.' I was surprised how easily this affectionate epithet rose to my lips. It was the first time I had called anyone dear for ten years or more.

Selina wept tears of blood. They stained her dress and left unsightly long red streaks on her deathly pale skin. 'Oh, Joanna, I'm so sorry I got you into this mess. If only I'd been more careful.'

There was a rustling movement from the darkened pews.

Selina groped inside her dress and held up the crucifix. I looked around me for a weapon. My eye fell on some spiky black iron candlesticks beneath a statue of Our Lady. But before I could seize these, a young woman emerged from the shadows. She was dark-skinned, with long black hair, and she was carrying a baby in one arm, while arranging her dress; I assumed she had been discreetly breastfeeding. 'I can help you,' she said gently to Selina. 'If you'll just hold the baby for me, please . . . '

Selina obeyed with alacrity. The baby waved its arms in her face and gurgled. 'Oh what a darling – choo choo,' she murmured.

The young woman hurried up the aisle and back, swinging a golden ball on three chains. 'This is used for asperges,' she said. 'For sprinkling holy water over the congregation. Gather the chains low down and you can direct the water accurately through these little holes. It won't hurt you,' she said, addressing Selina. 'That was only your fear. Holy water never harmed anyone. But it will vanquish your enemies, joined with my prayers for your safety. Hurry now!' and she took the baby back.

'But are we allowed – ?' Selina protested nervously at the door. 'The priest – won't he – ?'

The young woman smiled. 'I say what's allowed,' she said. 'It's my church. Light a candle to me next time you come here.'

Selina's sisters made a concerted lunge as we emerged, but the holy water ball got us through safely.

Vampire bat

A famous naturalist, on an expedition to collect rare species for his open-air zoo in the Channel Islands, determined to capture a vampire bat. He was travelling in a mountain-

41

ous district of South America, when he stopped to ask directions from an indigenous hillside farmer, scraping his precarious existence from the rocky terrain. The naturalist casually raised the subject of vampire bats. Yes, the hillside farmer knew of such creatures. Occasionally they took blood from his cattle. They had also been known to prey on sleeping human beings. Their razor-sharp teeth made only a small slit in the skin, through which they sucked nourishment, leaving the victim greatly weakened.

Encouraged by this information, the naturalist conceived the novel idea of using himself as bait. He built a high lookout post, and there he slept naked in the moonlight. But the vampire bat never came. Vampire bats are shy creatures, in habit finicky and particular. The naturalist was forced at last to admit failure and went away despondent. Months afterwards he learnt that the bite of the Argentinian blood bat, *Pipistrella sanguinea*, nearly always proves fatal, since the bat's teeth exude a substance that prevents blood from clotting. In the event of success, the naturalist would certainly have bled to death, being ignorant of the antidote, a certain leaf in the forest.

'By day Corinne Sanderson (22) works as a legal assistant for a big City firm. Expensive dental treatments have lengthened her upper canine teeth and she avoids garlicky foods. "Since word got around the office, I've not had any problems with sexual harassment," says Corinne. "Vampirism is a fun lifestyle option for young singles." '

'Vamping it up', feature on modern-day vampires in *Lunch Break* magazine, March 1990

Little-known facts about vampires

  * Vampires hate (vegetable) sugar and all artificial sugary substances. For Selina, drinking strawberry milkshake was a horrible form of self-violence and mortification, equivalent to a human being drinking sewage water.
  * A mortal being becomes a vampire on first tasting innocent blood. This may not be for decades. Thereafter, she remains the same age for eternity.
  * Sunlight is not harmful to vampires, although being night feeders, they often sleep during the day.
  * In type, vampires tend to be thoughtful and sensitive, often artistic.
  * They suffer badly from migraines and frequently have nervous breakdowns.
  * Virginia Woolf was a vampire. This fact has so far been assiduously concealed by her biographers. But why? It provides an invaluable key to interpretations of her work.
  * So was John Donne ('Mark but this flea and mark in this how little that which thou deny'st me is . . . ').
  * No one ever rated normal sex very highly after having been bitten by a skilled vampire. The bite imparts an extraordinary pleasure (I can vouch for this myself).

Selina's botched baptism had only one noticeable effect. As if in pity, or by way of compensation for her still-missing reflection/soul, the mirrors in my flat began singing to her. Whenever she looked searchingly, despairingly into, or even just walked past one. Often the air was filled with their beautiful, unearthly high voices.

We still slept in separate beds and I locked my door at night. I wanted her to feel safe. I have never yet trusted my own desires and she stirred depths I would rather not have remembered. Often in passing, in the middle of conversation, when she was laughing, I felt the urge to grab hold of her. But I stopped myself, conscious of being twenty years older, even though she was immortal.

One night we saw a television drama about Karen Carpenter, the talented young singer who died of anorexia. Selina watched the screen intently, leaning forward in her chair. During a moving reconciliation scene between Karen and her mother, several drops of blood rolled down Selina's cheeks. I passed her the box of tissues.

Her decline was rapid, through that autumn and into December. Though death, for her, was not a possibility, she reached that stage. And passed beyond it. During the daytime she looked her age. Several centuries old. At night, given a good strong moon and bright stars, she appeared again a young girl. But frail, unutterably frail. Empty of blood, drained.

I carried her into my bedroom, where the moon shone directly in at the window. She weighed nothing, it was like holding a skeleton. We lay together on the bed, in the moonlight, in one another's arms, and she told me stories. The mirrors sang softly. The faraway stars chimed like tiny bells.

Then she became unable to speak, even to move her lips. Her eyes turned glassy, empty.

In despair, I drove to the church of St Mary the Virgin at Southgate. The golden holy water ball was still rattling around in the boot of my car, that was my excuse for going back. My real purpose was to entreat the Virgin for help. To ask for mercy.

44

She wasn't there. Only the plaster statue. I lit a candle and said a prayer remembered from my childhood.

Hail holy Queen, mother of mercy
Hail our life, our sweetness and our hope
To thee do we cry, poor banished children of Eve
To thee do we send up our sighs, mourning and weeping
in this vale of tears
Turn then, most gracious advocate, thine eyes of mercy
towards us
And after this our exile . . .

I found myself crying, with the old feeling of not being heard, of praying into a vacuum.

Oh dear Lady, have mercy on Selina. She is innocent, gentle and good. Anyone can see that. So she's a vampire and she may have killed a few people. But that's in her nature, how can you blame her? You understand the need for a drink, don't you, Blessed Virgin? Remember the wedding at Cana, when you turned the water into strong red wine. And – you have saved the best wine till last, said the amazed guests.

I heard a faint hiss and opened my eyes. A painted green snake was curled around the plaster Virgin's feet; bright-eyed, with shining green scales. The Virgin was obviously fond of it – a favourite pet? – judging by the liberties it was allowed. As I watched, its gold tongue flickered in and out; then it uncurled and slithered rapidly away towards the church door.

Though I may be a lapsed Catholic, I can recognize a miraculous sign when I see one. I ran after the snake. Dusk was falling. I followed its metallic green flashing through the churchyard, down the main road, over several crossings, until it vanished into the Moon and Stars pub.

45

The Virgin Mary was serving behind the crowded bar, pulling pints. She looked harassed, her piled-up hair falling down in wisps. She wore a white T-shirt with a cartoon print; it said 'Oh my God, I left the baby on the bus'.

I battled my way to the front. When I tried to pay for my lager and lime she said, 'Forget it. Can't talk right now – see you later. I'm up to my eyeballs with these bastards.'

I found a seat near the dartboard. An old lady was playing darts with deadly accuracy, while sipping a Bloody Mary. Selina's mother. Her eyes flickered over me.

'Hello,' I said.

'So it's you,' she sneered. 'The mortal meddler. The half and halfer. The grave worm, that preys on decaying flesh. The sun-born leech, the parasite.'

'Sorry?'

She spat. I wiped blood off my face. It speckled the surface of my lager and lime. 'Do you mind?' I said feebly.

'Not so pretty now, is she?'

'Are you blaming me for – ? Listen,' I said, 'let's not waste time arguing. Selina's in a desperate – '

'She's my sweet daughter. I fed her with my own blood.'

'You also murdered her girlfriend.'

'So? I'm her mother, aren't I? With a mother's natural feelings. What else am I supposed to do?'

'Love her?'

'Of course I bloody love her. More than *you* ever will. Milksop mortal.'

'Are you jealous?' I said, my temper rising.

'Jealous of you? *You*, incapable and riddled with fears like a worm-shot corpse?'

'You old blood bag!' I shouted.

'Ladies, ladies . . . ' The Virgin Mary appeared between us, placing a restraining hand on Selina's mother's

46

shoulder. The old woman had drawn back her upper lip,
revealing two long and glistening canines. The Virgin bent
and whispered something in her ear. On the next instant,
to my surprise, the old bat vanished.

'Thank God,' I said feelingly.

'You just got on her wrong side. She's very nice really.'

'*Very nice?*'

'And wise. She's in my women's spirituality group. Pass
me that empty glass.'

Crone

General designation of the third of the Triple Goddess's
three aspects, exemplified by such figures as Kali the
Destroyer, Cerridwen the Death-dealing Sow, Atropos the
Cutter, Macha, Hecate, Hel, Eresh-Kigal, Morgan, Queen
of the Ghostworld, Queen of the Underworld, Queen of the
Shades, Persephone 'the Destroyer', etc . . . Her fearsome
character often had a 'virgin mother' side as well, because
her trinity of appearances was cyclic. It was said in the
East that true lovers of the Goddess must love her ugly
'destroyer' images as well as her beautiful ones.

The Women's Encyclopaedia of Myths and Secrets, Barbara
G. Walker

Balancing a tray of empty beer mugs the Virgin Mary
gazed at me, her glance sweet, loving and thoughtful.
Courage flowed into me with that long look; I knew what
I had to do.

I went home, walked into my bedroom where I had left
Selina. She'd gone. There in her place, lying on the bed,
was her mother.

Now I've seen dead people and dead was how she

looked   sunken eyelids   head tipped back   mouth a dark
hole   I sat down gingerly beside her   not a heartbeat   I
cupped her breast in my left hand, her shrunken old
breast   I did that with my own mother's body, left alone
with her open coffin in the visiting parlour   ancient ges-
ture of reverence   I am flesh of your flesh   the difference
being my mother's false teeth were taken out and her face
sort of collapsed, but here the teeth were very much *in
situ*   big white canines   all her strength in those
teeth   silver hair like Selina's, but stringy and thin with
bald patches   yellow skin cold, no blood in it   I am touching a dead thing   like a chicken before it goes in the
oven   I asked my mother for blessing   mother, you gave
me life   a life for a life   living with my mother was hell
on earth, but I made things right between us   I put my
wrist to the old woman's mouth   take me   her eyes flickered open, her mouth bit down on me   clamp   oh my
god   electric pain surges through my veins   what pos-
sessed me   some suicidal desire   love   she's got the main
artery   like a baby greedily sucking   blood dribbles from
the corners of her mouth   is this pain or exquisite
pleasure   and she's changing   changing   silver hair   a
pool of molten silver   face of a young girl   Selina   she
raises herself above me   I've collapsed on the bed   weak
as a baby   she clasps my wrist to stop the blood
spurting   Joanna, she says   I didn't intend this should
happen   not what I wanted   you understand don't you
Joanna, please don't die   darling, I reply faintly   self-
control admirable   sparing my heart's blood   most
unpleasant I'm sure it would have tasted   how are you
feeling   I love you, she says, live forever   and sweet
Virgin, into your hands I commend my immortal soul.

48

Yellow Bear

Linda Leatherbarrow

I'm six foot eleven and up here that's a problem. The
women are four foot ten. I yearn – okay lust – for someone
more proportionally compatible, less of a jigsaw puzzle;
someone with tender quivering thighs and resilient awe-
some breasts, a maiden in pursuit of Walt Disney's last
will and testament, cherry lips and a wiggle in her walk.
Inuit women are round. Sleepy eyes and well-wrapped,
cosy bodies. Pneumatic just doesn't come into it.

Remember that film, *Ice Cold in Alex*? A little stringy
bloke comes staggering out of the khaki desert, upper-
class English voice – sand dry. His fingers are swollen
with the heat, shiny with sweat so he can hardly hold out
the coin. Ice Cold in Alex, and here am I breaking out
a can from the fridge. It's minus twenty-eight degrees
centigrade and Baffin Island is dark. Dark day and night.
In the land of the welfare polar bear it's almost Christmas,
and I'm worrying Frank at the bar, saying, It's gotta be
cold, Frank, real cold. Can't stand lukewarm beer.

I've got a copy of the *National Star*, the one with a mock-
up photo of an alien with the headline 'My dead daughter
was fucked by spacemen and bore chocolate bunnies'. I'm
thumbing through looking for pics of Dolly Parton and
thinking of breaking out. Thinking of Civilization . . .

49

Galactic leather bikers, fugitive anarcho smut pedlars, mad mountain monks. Fantastic variety. Unimaginable up here except I'm imagining it and blowing my fuse, freaking out on stale porn that was smuggled up in the summer daylight.

Like everyone else, I'm waiting for the plane. We've run out of booze. Same thing every month. The plane tips down onto the snow, we drag the crates in here and get happy, very very happy, wildly deliriously happy on rye whisky, then one by one the Inuit leap onto their skidoos and blast off into the big night. Those guys can orientate themselves anywhere. If you or I set off into that deep purple haze we'd be gone. For a long time you can hear them whooping it up, hear the putt-putting of their engines on the snow. Crazy drunk till they keel over and sleep. This goes on for a week then there's no more whisky and it's back to square one. I'm waiting for my bottle of Glenfiddich then I'm going to curl up in my glorified tent and dream big lush dreams, pillow breasts and saucer nipples. Into the Valley of the Super Vixens while outside the black wind wails past the cabins and skids a thousand miles across the frozen sea.

Everything's shrunk to my dome and the Co-op Hotel. In the summer we get tourists, fishermen, bird fanciers, loonies in cut-offs (don't they read the brochure?), misinformed binocular trippers going out to Bylot Island to watch the birdies; but now we're into the big dark and there's just me, 117 locals, Frank who runs the hotel and Joe the dental technician. I'm the lawyer. Someone has to take on the oil companies and the gas johnnies.

I tap away at my typewriter, wearing the digit down into a bloody stump, waiting for the Co-op to fly in a computer; tap away, tossing off legal jargon straight into the jugular of Canadian capitalism. I love it and the Co-op pays me a fortune. Well, not exactly, but what is there to spend it on? I let it pile up in the bank.

Soon I'll get into property, buy a nice little house and rent it out to single teen mothers or neophyte table dancers. My eventual destination is premature retirement, cruising the blue but cold briny in a sixty footer while editing a fanzine devoted to the apocalyptic culture; interviewing ranters, cranks, meatless lentil saviours, and others in the flourishing undergrowth. Meanwhile I play crusading legal eagles, freezing my rocks off but breathing in the clean, clean air. Work for eight hours, kill time for ten, sleep for six. Must be outta my fucking mind. I could be walking the wet pavements of Soho or sliding down an alley in Amsterdam.

I guess I'm doing a good job – salvaging Inuit pride, getting them a better deal. They've all got consumer durables now: videos, washing machines, garbage compactors, deep freezes. It's TV suppers in the frozen north. All this stuff you read about the Inuit killing the narwhale for sustenance is just a load of shit. Don't you believe it. Unlimited quantities of narwhale tusks going to British buyers and Japanese, getting ground up into potions and aphrodisiacs. Controlled quota system my arse.

I'm going for a mocha milkshake. Not a burger-bar fishbone and chalk number but a mix-it-myself additive free special. The Co-op put an ice-cream parlour in the hotel last month. The kids sit around all day melting vanilla sundaes, cassatas, bombes, banana splits; any combination of three flavours for a dollar fifty. That's what we call entertainment, watching a slow dollop of strawberry ice-cream fall down a long-stemmed glass while outside the wind cuts you to shreds and the snow's so crisp it squeaks. It's night, dusky midday dark and the polar bears are hibernating and so am I. Dug into American TV. Sitting on a barstool waiting.

I've ordered some tapes. They'd better be on that plane. Tina Turner and the lovely Madonna of the conical corsets. I used to be into punk, heavy metal. Motorhead and Girls' School, the Slits. Before that it was Jimi Hendrix . . . Electric Ladyland. Lovely sleazy clubs, sticky floors, strobe lights, doormen built like Sumo wrestlers, the Fabulous Marlene. She sat on my lap once and kissed me and everyone knew she was a man but on my lap she looked tiny. Now I'm thinking of cities, of bookshops, London in the sixties when Don and I ran a magazine called *Freedom*. I remember going into a pub in Guildford with a black balloon, a sparkler coming out of the end, and screaming *BOMB!* Don got three months.

I came straight back to Canada, took up law, then found that the offices in Toronto have carpets on the walls. 'The land of the bland.' I lived in a wooden shack at the east end of Toronto Island, squatting and commuting to work on the ferry. Great place, but in the summer it was hotching with tourists, and the city was getting bigger, taller and taller by the day. The motor city of the north. I looked up Eskimo in a book in the library, *The Canadian Nation* it was called – nothing. I looked up Inuit – nothing. First I went to Yellowknife, then here. Four years later, I'm flat on my back on my futon, wallowing in literature of a less than salubrious nature.

In the morning the plane arrives, dropping out of a black sky and rustling down on skis. Lights slewing, shadow sharp. A new pilot and no Glenfiddich, no tapes. Unbelievable chaos. Crates piled up all over the snow. Shouting. Torches. Too cold to look. My nose almost dropping off.

The roar of skidoos everywhere, slamming up the Sound, echoing off the ice.

I'm in the hotel kitchen with Ana Akulujuk and she's breaking open a crate of French wine. The writing on the crate says Frobisher Bay but who cares? Ana holds a bottle beautifully in a white napkin, pours slowly, delicately, and we chink glasses. Ana is the hotel cook. She's dinky and dimpled and smells of beef tallow. She's sixteen, her hair is black and tied back, and she's wearing a plastic bib-front apron that says BOSS. She decides we ought to eat. When going on a bender, she says, it's important to line the stomach. I watch her wield the frying pan and she's smiling. So am I. We sit on the floor, our backs to the big fridge, and tipple down the wine. We're lapping it up. The pilot comes in and we play checkers, moving cans of soup over the floor tiles, and he's even drunker than we are. Ana is talking about the South and I'm listening. After a little while the pilot leaves and Ana takes my hand.

I wake up back in my dome and she's with me. There's a pile of greasy cold pancakes and a lemon on the table. My dome has a double skin and the inside one is usually covered with pictures, inspirational lovelies, stuff I don't care to think about now. The walls are blank and there's a pile of paper scraps on the floor. I look at this for a moment but we're naked and it's the first time in months that I haven't slept in socks, thermal leggings and my Newfie fisherman's jumper. It's the first time in years that I've slept with someone else. I get back swiftly under the duvet and cuddle up, shit scared and desperate, praying she'll stay. I think about the porn mags concealed in the cabinet with my clothes; think about snuff movies I haven't seen; think about a scheme I once had – how the video stuff cost me a fortune, and the girls smoked too much pot and passed out on the sofa like a pair of happy lovers, and all I got in return was a black suspender belt they left in the bathroom. Think in a panic. Try not to. Think about the hair of the dog. Put my head out again but the bottle is empty. Think about the dirt between my toenails, the grey hairs on my chest, the lack of hairs on my head.

She's generating enough heat for two. I touch her slowly and slide my hand down over her skin, then she wakes and rolls over and sits on my chest, dangling her little spiky breasts in my face, and I can't deny she's beautiful. No more than four foot ten and beautiful. 'As founder member of the West Baffin women's group,' she says, 'I'm putting you straight. The Arctic needs cleaning up.'

It's a shock. I haven't adjusted. She's round-shouldered, she's hairy, she's sweaty and she stuffs her neat little foot in my mouth and I nibble her toes. Grateful.

She comes back the next day, pale and wobbly with lack of sleep and a hangover to match mine – and legs that ache from fitting themselves round my long body. She tells me that. She says doing it with me is a form of yoga, like hip stretches. If she keeps it up she expects she'll soon be able to sit cross-legged on the floor with her knees touching the ground like the yogi do.

She puts a wall-hanging on the wall. A black felt square with bright orange and yellow cut-out felt figures carefully sewn on with tiny stitches. Hunters, a polar bear on its hind legs, another on all-fours, two men lying flat on the snow, guns pointing ahead, jumping dogs, a sledge. It reminds me of Fuzzy Felt. I had rheumatic fever as a kid and Fuzzy Felt saved my life. I'd move the little pieces around for hours, making up stories. I had the basic box but best of all was Circus Fuzzy Felt. There was a bear on its hind legs just like this one.

We spend the whole day banging about my dome, on the floor, in the bed, on the table. We do it until I don't think I'll ever stand up again and she laughs and does it again for herself, me lying next to her, holding her, feeling her going stiff and shivery and warm at the same time, then letting go in a noisy little spasm that makes me hard again. I'd no idea. Just no idea.

I feel privileged, milk-drunk like a baby, and wide open at the same time. Like the whole nasty mess I've waded through all my life, that rabid mix of schlock and Mega-City Terminators; the whole caboodle, Judge Dread and Ms Lenin, discipline lessons given for ideological deviants, all gone, blasted into a black hole and I'm up in here in the Arctic, somehow on the edge of everything and ahead of everything. Out there the forces of capitalism are hitting the elements with a vengeance and imploding into the night, but inside my dome I'm wrapped up in Ana's arms, empty-headed and blissfully spent. Humble. She proceeds to fill in the gaps in my education, lies beside me explaining why all men are shits, how pornography abuses women, how rape is a collective male crime, and patriarchy enslaves. I take it all in. She's firmly in control. I know it. She knows it. No question.

There are very few guests in the hotel. Just a few men for a contracting company come to see about building a fishing camp in the summer. Ana goes to cook their meals and I try and work while she's gone. I feel as if my mind is full of sunshine and dust motes, even though I can hardly remember what sunshine looks like. Ana's efficiency doesn't seem to be impaired. She makes them the usual caribou steaks, french fries, double eggs, raisin muffins, thick brown coffee and chocolate brownies, and in between washing up and cooking she gives me lectures while sliding wetly on my thighs.

In addition, she's mad about barbecues on Bondi Beach, picnics in the English countryside, espresso coffee sipped slowly on an Italian piazza, swimming pools in Los Angeles. Wouldn't it be nice, she says, and she's off. For hours. She can literally talk for hours. Transcribing it from the TV onto another screen right in front of our eyes while the duvet folds around us, a tent within a tent. Nothing outside but ice and snow and months of glacial night.

Oh yeah, I say, go South. Hit the donut galleries. Take in the malls. Cruise the 401, twelve lanes of freeway fun. Eighteen at the intersections. I tickle her stomach but she frowns. Shit, I say, in Edmonton, Alberta, there's a mall so big they've got a man-made lake under glass; you can sail, surf, swim, laze on imported sand, sail in pirate ships, dive in a real submarine. They've got four, maybe five submarines, more than the entire Canadian navy. Is that what you want? She looks sulky and I change tack, conjure up poison clouds of benzine, dioxin water. And then Beach Culture. Faecal waters slimy with sun-tan oil and belly-up fish. But she won't listen. She imagines herself in a shady café; imagines artists, actors, serious radical feminists, ultra chic. Imagines cicadas chirping, poets, playwrights – God knows. Saatchi and Saatchi and the moguls of Hollywood have done her head in.

The plane comes back. This time the crates are the right ones and we're all happy drunk again, twice in the same month. I'm in the hotel listening to Frank talking to the contractors about fishing records. A twelve-pound four-ounce char on a sixteen-pound class tippet on a fly rod. World record. That means big business, he says, and they nod. I'm spouting on about how we should turn the hotel into a parka factory and other mega-buck schemes, how tourists mean death and look what they've done to the Med, when I notice Ana's not around any more. I stagger back to my dome and take stock, on the way noting that the plane has hightailed it. I put two and two together and come across my empty cash box; 900 dollars vamoosed.

At first I'm angry, imagining her in a shiny new mall taking the Pepsi challenge, shaking hands with a fibre-glass promo-dwarf, buying a twenty-two-carat identity bracelet and a pair of pink and white kangaroo-skin trainers. Then I realize I'm not giving her credit. This is a bright girl.

She's left me the wall hanging. I sit on my bed and stare at it. After a while I figure out it was worth it. Art's expensive and this is genuine, hand-sewn. The sort those smart-arsed galleries on Yorkville would kill for; along with antler and horn carvings, ivory and whalebone.

The yellow and orange figures are running together in front of my eyes and I look at that polar bear standing on its hind legs and I think, What the hell? That yellow bear represents the best days of my life. I stagger back to the hotel and get blind.

I still have the clean air, thousands and thousands of clean cubic feet. Sweet as apple juice.

Fun Fotos

Helen Sandler

I put on the black tights, white blouse, the short skirt and the spangled shoes. I wear blue eyeshadow, blossom-pink lipstick.

No one can tell in the dark, I'm sure. They just see another woman pass by, bag swinging from her shoulder.

Tilly tipped up the envelope and a dried turd fell on to the conveyor belt. She shrieked but the supervisor just laughed. 'Perk of the job,' she said, pulling a face. 'Get it back! It'll be in the lab in seconds.'

Skipping quickly down the line, Tilly lunged at the turd and slipped its envelope under it as if it were a spider on the floor at bedtime.

It *was* bedtime. But she was in the Fun Fotos processing factory in Salford, in mid-season. That meant thousands of rolls of holiday film, and the factory running twenty-four hours a day, on three shifts. Tilly felt as if she were working all three of them. She was not a Night Person.

It was time for her break, so she dropped the turd into the bin and headed for the sandwich shop. The shop was the domain of Jess, a tall dark woman in her late thirties, with an unusual, large-boned face and deep-seeing eyes. Tilly was first in the queue, arriving just ahead of the midnight bleeper that signified the official start of the break. She was greeted with Jess's lipstick smile and a corned beef sandwich.

'You look like you could use a cup of tea, love.'

'I'm knackered,' Tilly replied, 'and some bastard sent a piece of dogshit in his film envelope and it's just about the last straw.'

Jess handed her a cup of tea and looked carefully at her. 'You need a good cry, don't you?'

'How can you tell?'

'I'm just very clever. Go and break the first rule of hygiene.'

'You what?'

'Eat your butty in the bog. Have a weep at the same time and you'll have got everything out of the way in your first break. That's 80p for your grub and seven pound fifty for the advice, please.'

Working nights made Tilly feel permanently premenstrual. As she sat on the toilet with her sandwich on her bare left knee and her tea on top of the disposal unit, the tears flooded out in exhausted despair. She wanted to go home. But if she took to *sleeping* by night instead of opening orange envelopes, she'd have no job to replace this one. She could dye her spiky hair back to normal from peroxide white, stop wearing what her mother called 'men's clothes' and start wearing 'pretty clothes', and go for a job in a shop. Or she could tour the factories again through the long summer days, looking for casual work. A fortnight's work, maybe, then a stint on the dole, then a few days in a stinking hot paint factory. She'd been through it all before. At least this was a permanent job . . .

There was a knock on the cubicle door.

'Tilly?'

'Just a sec.' She wiped her hand across her face, placed

the sandwich on top of the plastic cup, and pulled up her jeans. She slid back the lock and Jess swung inside and stood against the door.

'Thought I'd come and cheer you up,' she said.

There was just time to think of all the stories about the married women who think any dyke is ready for action any time, before Jess's long arms encircled her and, jammed between the door and the toilet, they kissed with all the passion of the middle of the night.

I walk through Albert Square as the clock on the town hall strikes twelve. The night buses glow orange as they make their way round town. A gang of youths stare at me, on their way to Oxford Road perhaps. It is enough for me to walk and be seen, even to be stared at. I do not need the pubs and clubs to excite me.

A police car screams up Cross Street and I hide in a shop doorway. I have heard what they can do to me, what they've done to others for nothing more than walking the streets in clothes like mine. I keep away from them.

Jimmy Cardogan lay in his bunk in D-Wing with his radio earpiece in place and his face up close to the wall, to make out Debbie's photo in the dark. He imagined her hearing the DJ announcing his request as she lay in bed with a book; pictured her kissing the photo of him that she kept by the bed.

'Lonely Without You' began to play and Jimmy put a hand to his heart, which was beating too fast for two reasons: Mike Sentry had read out his letter for the whole of Manchester to hear; and he could see Debbie so clearly that for a beautiful, terrible moment he believed he was back home.

61

Debbie Cardogan had not told Jimmy that she had started working nights at Fun Fotos. She had not told the factory that her husband was in Strangeways. So when the message came over the tannoy that Jimmy was 'missing her badly and sends all his love', she didn't wait to hear which soppy song the great daft twit had ordered. She gathered her dignity and went to the toilet.

There was a snogging noise coming from the middle cubicle. Debbie lowered herself heavily to her knees and peered under the door at a pair of strappy sandals and two Doctor Marten boots.

Hoping to make someone feel more embarrassed than the radio broadcast had made *her*, she hauled herself back up and called, 'Excuse me, is there a man in the toilet?'

Two sets of female giggles and a 'no' came back in reply.

'Want to join us, love?'

'No I don't,' Debbie shouted. 'I came to the bogs for a bit of peace, not a lesbian orgy. Who's in there?'

The door opened.

'Jess! What are you doing to that youngster?'

They grinned at her. 'This is Tilly,' said Jess, 'and she's old beyond her years.'

'I know who she is, and she's due back on shift. You're a bad influence.' Debbie placed her hands staunchly on her hips and tried to look as if she meant it. As a supervisor she was supposed to reprimand bad conduct. But she had not foreseen dykey goings-on in the Ladies when she practised telling people off in front of her bathroom mirror.

Still, it worked. Tilly straightened her face, said, 'Sorry, I hadn't noticed the time,' and left.

Debbie looked at Jess and felt tears bubbling behind her eyes.

'Is summat up with you, love?' Jess asked, invoking the friendship they'd had as kids and lost along the way.

'Oh Jess ... everything's so bloody difficult.' Debbie swallowed hard and launched with relief into her story. 'Our Jimmy's in the nick for a washing machine, a microwave and a deep freeze. He seems to think of it as a kind of romantic separation. But the truth of it is that he's left me with no money – that's why I took this bloody job.

'I didn't really want to work nights, but I have to 'cos I'm keeping the lad home from school.'

'Why?'

'Because they won't let him eat a banana at playtime. The teacher says it's too messy. I decided it was time for some parent power – not just for our Jason, but for all the parents who want to send their kids to school with whatever fruit they like.'

'So have they all rallied round?'

'No.'

'And where is he when you're at work?' asked Jess.

'He stays with his nan. She's fine with him when he's asleep, but as soon as he's conscious she starts to tell him what an evil man his father is, and how little boys who are naughty will get locked up like Daddy.'

'So his dad ... ' Jess began, trying to get a full picture.

'Yeah?'

'Well, did he rob a warehouse or summat?'

'Oh no, he only got those three things – they were for my kitchen. He nicked them from the Rumbelows closing-down sale. He just wheeled them out of the shop and into the van, one at a time. The place was chaos, so he says – everything was half-price and most of it was reserved by the dentist on the next floor. Dozens of people were fighting over what was left and no one was watching our Jimmy. Except the video cameras.'

'Well, it was nice of him to try.'

I take a tour of the streets around the coach station where the gays go. Sometimes I see others like myself but tonight there are only a few rentboys and gaggles of clubgoers.

The women are not dressed like me. They wear jeans and T-shirts or leather jackets and glance meanly at me. I look away.

I go to the coach station to use the Ladies. When I come out there is a man outside the Gents staring at me.

'All right, love?'

I nod and move away but he calls after me, 'In a hurry are you? Wouldn't you like to spend a bit of time with me?'

I turn back to see on what level he is mocking me, whether he actually wants me or not. I know as I turn that I should have kept on walking. A uniformed policeman comes towards us.

'How's your Mac anyway?' asked Debbie, as Jess handed her a restorative cup of tea.

'Wouldn't like to say, love. He *thinks* too much for my liking, always has. I can't watch *Coronation Street* without him explaining the underlying message to me. He talks more and more like a nightschool teacher.'

'Well, just be thankful he has a brain and knows how to use it,' said Debbie. 'My Jimmy's a few butties short of a British Rail buffet.'

Strangeways is on fire.

It started with the banging and shouting that Jimmy often heard at night, men penned in and calling from cell to cell, chanting, swearing, until the screws came round and opened doors and shouted back, and a young lad's voice shrieked out, 'Let us out of here, Jesus Christ!' and smoke came into Jimmy's cell.

Fuller jumped out of the top bunk before Jimmy was

64

clear what was happening, and then Mallone was banging on the door and yelling at the screws and Jimmy got up and joined him.

'Get over to A-Wing,' said the officer as he unlocked the door. Men were pelting past and Jimmy saw Braithwaite knock one of the screws to the ground with a punch to the jaw.

'Come on, you silly bugger,' called Fuller, 'we're going up on the roof.'

'This is Piccadilly Radio news at 1am. A riot has broken out tonight at Strangeways jail. It's believed inmates started a fire in D Wing but it's not yet known whether anyone is injured. Men can be seen on the roof of the prison. Our reporter Jeremy West, is on the scene.

'Soon after midnight tonight . . . '

The factory radio cut out and a nasal voice whined over the tannoy: 'Jess McDonald, Jess McDonald, telephone call, please come to the office. That's a phone call for Jess McDonald in the office now, please.'

The report came back on. Jess and Debbie exchanged worried looks and Jess hurried away, up concrete stairs and into a small, scruffy room where a young woman pointed at a telephone before going back to her library book.

Jess picked up the receiver.

'Mrs McDonald?'

'Yes.'

'My name's Sergeant Redmond, at Bootle Street police station.'

'Oh aye.'

'We've got your husband here. Would you be able to come and pick him up?'

I sit in the cell in a blanket. They have taken away my

clothes and tell me that my wife will come to collect me. They find this amusing. I have told them what I know to be best – someone more experienced once explained, stopping me in the street to list these warnings before moving on.

So I have said that I cannot help it, that I feel a need to wear these clothes and that I frequently telephone a helpline for counselling.

In fact I do nothing of the sort. I am surprised to find how easily I can lie to these men, in spite of – or perhaps because of – the fear. They are mostly young, there are many of them, and they all watched me undress.

'Is he all right? What happened?' Tilly amazed herself with these generous questions. She really wanted to tell Jess to leave Mac in the cells for the day and come back to her place.

'I'm not sure.' Jess looked away from them and said, 'He puts on frocks and suchlike and goes out like that at night. They said they'd mistook him for a prostitute.'

Tilly thought she might laugh.

'Y'mean you knew he was doing it?' Debbie said.

'Oh aye, yeah, he's been doing it for years, at least. But what am I to do?' Jess glanced around the deserted entrance hall and back at the two women. 'He's all right, you know. He's never done me any harm and he's kept nowt from me. He's just a bit weird. But who isn't?' She smiled at Tilly.

Debbie said decisively, 'I'm coming with you.'

'There's no need, love, honest. I've to go home first and fetch him a decent set of clothes, the whole thing will take forever.'

'No, really, I want to come. Any road, the police might

know summat about our Jimmy. And we could go past the
jail and have a quick look on the way.'

'What size is he, Jess?' asked Tilly suddenly.

'You what, love?'

'Your husband. What size clothes does he take?'

'Oh . . . sort of middling.'

Tilly gestured at her own outfit; enormous T-shirt, baggy
jeans. 'Medium menswear?' she asked with a grin.

'Aye, I suppose.'

'Well then, I'll swap him. Debbie, sign me out.'

Debbie glared at her for insubordination.

It was exciting on the roof but it was also getting cold and
probably dangerous. Fuller kept shouting with the full
force of his lungs. Things like, 'We'll burn the whole fucking place to the ground,' and, 'Bring your cameras in here
and see for yourself. It's a shit-hole.'

Most of the others were ignoring him. He was waving
his fist excitedly and his large frame moved in a quick
rhythm as if he were hitting someone. Jimmy wondered if
anyone could hear. He could see the lights of the television
people but they were a long way off.

It was strange being outdoors in the dark. Not that it
was very dark with the searchlights on them, but if he lay
down and squinted he could see the stars.

Once, he and Debbie had camped on Kinder Scout. They
were just kids really. He woke up at dawn and crawled
out of the tent and he was – well, on top of the world.

The Hooped Skirt

Robyn Vinten

The moon was just past full and slightly misty. Karen drove as fast as she could down Wightman Road. Beating a man away from the lights – he tooted angrily – she gave him the fingers and laughed. She loved racing round London when everyone else was asleep, the windows down and the radio on full. On a night like this she could do anything. She was coming from a party which she had really enjoyed. She had spent the whole evening in the kitchen, keeping everyone laughing, telling jokes and doing Thatcher impersonations with the washing-up brush. She had even been propositioned.

She parked the car and went into the house by the back door. The two women she shared with were away, but tonight it didn't worry her. She could watch a late film, put the stereo on really loud and dance naked in the lounge, or she could just go up to bed. She took off her shirt as she went through the kitchen, and left her shorts by the loo. She stopped to admire the moon again before pulling her bedroom curtains, and saw there was someone in the garden.

She pulled back from the window, her heart pounding. Not sure if she had imagined it, she peered round the edge of the window. There was a man looking up at her. She

69

recognized the glasses: it was the man in the car she had beaten away from the lights.

She was shaking, her breathing was too fast, she realized how little she was wearing. It took her a moment before she could move, then she went to the phone and dialled 999. They seemed to take forever to answer. She tried to breathe normally. When she was put through to the police she didn't know what she was going to say. The word 'prowler' came from nowhere. They said they would be there as soon as they could.

She sat for a moment after hanging up, wondering what to do. Then, carefully, staying out of sight, she went into the other room that overlooked the back garden. The man was at the back door, his hand on the door handle. She prayed that she had remembered to lock it. He moved away. She ducked back from the window. Suddenly she was very angry, she wanted to open the window and throw things at him, rush downstairs and scream at him. She wanted to grab a knife and stick it in his face. But she was too scared to move.

She sat in the middle of the room, hugging herself, shivering. She wanted to put some clothes on, but she would have to go back into her room, where he might see her. How dare anyone make her feel so frightened she couldn't go into her own room.

She reached for a dressing gown hanging on the back of her flatmate's door. There was a noise downstairs – not very loud, but a noise. She froze, straining to hear. There was silence, then she heard it again, the barest creak. She tiptoed to the window, but she couldn't see the man.

She heard another noise, closer. She looked round the room for something to hit him with; something heavy to smash his brains in. She picked up the table lamp, and with shaking hands unplugged it. Then slowly and quietly she moved to the door. She edged her way to the top of the stairs and carefully looked over the rail. There was no one in the kitchen. Breathing hard she started down the stairs. Before she was halfway down a shadow crossed the front door. She stopped dead.

The doorbell sounded, alarmingly loud after the silence. She stood, not sure what to do. The bell sounded again, then the letterbox rattled. A woman's voice. It was the police.

She rushed down, still holding the lamp. A plainclothed policewoman pushed through the half-opened door and flashed her ID.

'Where is he?'

'The back.'

The woman shouted something to someone outside. She asked Karen for a description.

'He wore glasses.'

'And . . . '

'It was dark. I couldn't see well.'

'Tall? Short? Black? White?'

'Average.'

The WPC talked into her walkie-talkie.

'Can I just . . . ?' Karen felt naked. The WPC nodded. She hurried upstairs and grabbed her flatmate's dressing gown. When she was putting the lamp back she caught a glimpse of a head bobbing over the fence. For a moment she thought it was another prowler, then she realized it was a policeman. She nearly laughed.

The policewoman asked her more questions, none of which she could answer properly. She felt very stupid.

'You should wear some more clothes around the house, or pull your curtains. You live here alone?'

'No, but the others are away.'

'He's probably miles away by now. Ring us immediately if you see him again.'

The policewoman left.

'But wait!' Karen wanted to say. 'Stay for a cup of tea. I'm scared, I don't want to be alone.'

To calm herself she checked the doors. The front door, through which the policewoman had just left, then the french windows, shut and locked. The kitchen window, and the back door, all bolted. She went back up to her room and pulled the curtains quickly. The garden was empty, the moon had set. She climbed into bed and did crosswords until she couldn't keep her eyes open any more. Then putting the book carefully beside her bed, she fell asleep.

Her door opened slowly, inch by inch, in slow motion, then through it came a man. He stood there in the half-light. She squinted at him; it was Sylvester Stallone. He came towards her like he was swimming underwater, his hands outstretched as if to strangle her.

She felt on the table beside her bed and her hands closed around a giant pair of scissors. She leapt out of bed and lunged at him, stabbing him with the scissors again and again, all in slow motion. He fell over like a mannikin, all in one piece. She kicked his head, slow and hard, then she jumped on it, again and again. He looked surprised, hurt; not physically, but as if he couldn't understand why she was doing this to him.

She shouted and screamed at him. She was wearing a wooden frame; like a hooped skirt, only it was huge. It was filling up with her anger and her hate. There was never going to be room for it all.

Even before she woke, she knew it had been a dream. Her head was splitting, and her throat was tight with unshed

72

tears. The violence of the dream left her feeling sick. She looked at her watch: 6:30 am. She lay back and the tears started to flow, across her cheeks and into her ears.

She got up to go to the loo, and nearly tripped over the body.

She stood for ages looking down at it. There was a bloody smear on the carpet, and one hand was stretched out, like he was trying to push himself away. The eye she could see was bruised. To get to her door she would have to step over it. She backed off and sat at her desk. It was getting light outside, the birds were singing. She didn't want to, but she kept staring at the body.

Then, slowly, she stood up and carefully walked to the door, stepping over the body, trying not to touch it. She walked down the hall to the phone, and with the care of a drunk trying to appear sober she dialled 999 again. When she was put through to the police it took her a moment before she could speak, and then she had to repeat it because they couldn't hear her.

'There's a body in my room.'

She remembered the story of Bluebeard and his murdered wives, and how as a child she had thought 'body' meant your arms and legs fell off if you were killed.

She sat at the top of the stairs. From where she was she could see one of the man's feet. No matter how hard she stared at it, it didn't move. She felt completely empty, no emotions. No anger, no hate, no fear, no physical sensation. Just her eyes and the man's foot.

The doorbell rang, making her jump. It took her a moment to work out what was going on. She tried to stand, but it felt too dangerous. The bell rang again, and then again, louder. She somehow got down the stairs to the front door, just to shut them up. The noise was too terrible.

For some reason she had been expecting the same WPC,

but it was a man in uniform. She couldn't answer any of his questions, just pointed up the stairs. Three or four other officers pushed past her, taking the stairs two at a time. They were too big, making too much noise. The officer asking her questions was standing too close. She could only shake her head.

An ambulance arrived, its siren going. More people came into the house. They ushered her into the lounge and shut the door. Alone, she started to shake. All the things she hadn't been feeling before came rushing in on her. Up from the pit of her stomach. She threw up in the fireplace.

The door opened behind her, a woman in uniform came in. She looked at Karen in disgust and left again. There was vomit down the front of Karen's T-shirt. The policewoman came back with some clothes and thrust them at her, then watched her get changed. They were Karen's flatmate's clothes. They were too small, but Karen put them on anyway. She folded the T-shirt and put it in the fireplace. When she had finished the policewoman took her firmly by the elbow, led her out the front door and into a waiting police car.

She still dreamed about men, not the Stallone of that first dream, but men with big boots and shiny buttons, whispering what they were going to do to her when they got her alone. Men in wigs, looking down at her, telling her she should be locked up and the key thrown away. Paranoid, the psychiatrist (male) had called her. Karen had laughed. 'Showing no remorse,' he had added.

She still dreamed of the wooden frame, but it was full of water or fire or earth. 'A good sign,' her therapist (female) said. She told her to plant flowers in it. Karen was trying, she really was trying.

Chrysanthemum

Pushpa Sellers

I am going to give birth to the saviour and here they are
trying to murder me. I have to phone my husband because
it is not safe for me here. I run to the phone and dial O.
He will come in his white spaceship to save me. The nurses
grab the phone and wind the cord round my neck. 'Don't
murder me, I am essential to the salvation of the world.'
They hold me down and inject me with Chlorpromazine to
make me sleep. But I am still aware; they only think I'm
sleeping. I must hang on. The old woman opposite me is
dying. I smell it in the wilting chrysanthemums. I know
that when she dies, my child will be born, her spirit living
on in him. 'No,' the voice whispers, 'your father's soul will
live in him.' But Daddy's not dead. 'He will be. And,' the
voice whispers, 'you die.' Sand is being sprinkled over me,
the moon is full. A breeze ruffles my hair lightly. I can
feel it but I cannot move. They are covering me with sand
and soon I will not be able to say anything. My mouth will
be full of sand.

The woman at the far end is evil. Satan with his claws in
the shape of an arthritic old woman. I know, but I try to
ignore her casually, letting her think that I have been
fooled. I am frightened but I will not let her see. I must

keep control. When I stop concentrating everything dies. I hold the strings to all these lives. If I shake my foot too hard, the nuclear bomb attached to it will come unstuck. It will fall and explode. Fools. They didn't know I had that power.

We play hopscotch. She keeps winking at me. 'I know and you know,' she says. I wonder just how much she actually knows. There is blood on my nightdress, bright red blood. 'Only I know and you know.' When I look at her again her eyes are strange, a transparent yellow. She is not human. She must be from another planet. And where is my husband when I need him? I run to the phone and dial O. The nurses put me back to bed. Injection.

The strip lights are switched off. Everything is real now in the dim lamplight. Women float around in the blue underwater world, speaking in whispers. Moving from bed to bed, they heal the wounds that have been gashed open by men with their flickering metallic instruments. The bed gently rocks to the rhythm of the waves and if you listen carefully you can hear the silent song of the sea. A map is projected on to the ceiling, the colours vivid and sharp. Sri Lanka swells, turning a bright shade of purple as the other countries pale into insignificance. Over to the right Japan pulsates, a breathtaking mauve. India leaps out, but only for a moment, and then England, a rich violet. The land masses of Asia, America, Europe and the Middle East push and shove, squeezing each other aside, jostling for attention. But my triangle is complete. My three islands float serenely in their seas, confidently purple.

A doctor approaches. He is so thin that his skull is clearly

76

defined. I look at his hands and legs and see that they are just as skeletal. He is wearing a surgical mask above which his eyes bulge, prominent in their sockets. He's carrying what looks like a large hacksaw. 'I must remove your appendix,' he says. 'My appendix has already been taken away.' I reply. 'Then I'll remove something else,' he says, coming closer and raising the blade. 'No, please go away. Please leave me alone.' He walks away.

There is a man climbing up and through the window. He holds a knife which glints in the moonlight. I know he belongs to the National Front. 'Black and white, let's unite. Smash the National Front,' I cry, but the nurses carry on knitting silently, an unearthly grin on their faces. All I need do is shut my eyes and everything will stop. But what if I can't restart it? I will have to take the risk.

When I open my eyes it is morning. The woman doctor who I like is smiling into my face. 'How are you feeling?' she asks. 'Can I have some blood?' She leans towards me and I can now see that her face is green and her fangs have appeared. 'No,' I shout, pulling the blanket over my head. 'No no no.' After a while I carefully peer out. Everything is quiet. The doctor has disappeared.

There are twelve at dinner tonight. I sit at the head of the table all in white. Pauline wears pink and sits on my left. We have already started when the thirteenth woman comes to the table and sits at the other end. She is wearing a shimmering red satin robe. I am frightened and go back to bed.

We sit in the television room and watch the news. They're telling us about the new Pope who has been appointed.

The news is being read in Polish. It must be because the new Pope is Polish. I look around and notice that they are all speaking in Polish. It must be the new official language. The room gradually empties. Pauline and I sit on. I hold her hand and she tells me her problems. She cries. When her tears are dry she tells me she has second sight. 'I know you do too,' she says.

That night I get into Pauline's bed, which is on my left. 'I can't sleep in my own bed tonight,' I tell her. 'Something terrible will happen. That woman opposite will die . . . I know she'll die.' The smell of chrysanthemums is over-powering. Paulines strokes my hand and tells me not to worry. 'I'll protect you, darling.' She winks. I should have known that her wink meant betrayal. I am doomed to another night of horror. Then they all start appearing. Mary and Robin. John and Susie. It is a masquerade. That was all that it had ever been. I laugh. 'Okay. I know it's you, the game's over.' But they all persist in the masquerade. On and on. Nothing is what it seems. They all wear masks but their true identities are ill-concealed.

My mother lies in a bed across the ward. I know she is dead so I look away. But I can see her from the corner of my eye. She doesn't recognize me. She wears a pained expression, her eyes glazed. I look away and when I turn back she is gone.

My husband comes to visit me the next evening. He smiles and I smile back. 'You don't need your glasses any more. Hold my hand and your third eye will open. We can see. You see? We can see.' I take his glasses off and we sit holding hands. He asks me questions but I don't reply. We are together and that is all that matters.

'I'll call you tomorrow,' he says as he gets ready to go.

'No, I'll contact you,' I say. It's only after he's gone that I realize the significance of what I've said. He will never call me. I must call him.

I hear the jangle of keys and I know I will be locked up. I must escape.

The morning sun streams through the windows. I bathe and smile, clean and cooperative. 'May I go for a walk? I'm feeling so much better and it's such a lovely day.' To my surprise, the doctor says yes. I smile politely. 'Thank you.' Underneath my smiling mask my mind ticks away. Calculating. Have I got enough money? Do I have my husband's number? I must get to him before it's too late.

The sky is already darkening. The planes are approaching. Any minute the bomb will fall and we must be together. Must find a phone. Must find a phone. Please God don't let me be too late. 'He's not in today,' the receptionist says. I phone again. 'I'm sorry, your husband's not here today.' But I know she's lying. I want to ring again but I haven't got any more money, and I know it's too late anyway. I must face facts. We must die apart. We are solitary on this earth. We are born alone and we must die alone. My heart is heavy. The sky darkens and I am lost. I sit on the curb and a traffic warden directs me to the hospital. I sit in the waiting room; a room full of people unaware of their approaching death. The thought depresses me and I return to the ward. I am cold so I get into bed. I may as well be asleep when the bomb falls. I shut my eyes . . .

Lupercal

Frances Gapper

'Beware, his mind told him, of people who have in the course of their lives neither taken part in an orgy nor gone through the experience of childbirth, for they are dangerous people ...'

Isak Dinesen, *Seven Gothic Tales*

The arrival of wolves in Stoke Newington, a fashionable area of north-east London, did not at first cause widespread panic, or even much concern. Although some people worried about house prices, a general stagnancy in the property market made it difficult to judge if these were affected. Also, Stoke Newington is full of psychotherapists, who refused to believe in the wolves as objective reality, doubting even the evidence of their own eyes. Thus lycantherapy developed, a complex science, and many profound theses and articles were written. My friend Alice, who was training to be a child psychotherapist, presented a special paper to the Tavistock Clinic: 'Wolves in Our Waking Dreams: a Study of Mass Paranoia in Stoke Newington'.

I congratulated myself secretly on living in Tottenham, next to a nice park with no wolves in it. Alice lives near

Abney Park Cemetery, a hauntingly atmospheric place, with its fallen tombstones overgrown with ivy, its family graves and those of possible lovers, a war memorial commemorating whole streets of people, a stone lion outstretched on its keeper's grave and the stone angels, some with human faces. Here the wolves congregated and might easily be observed, padding in and out of the ruined chapel, peering around gravestones, playing with their cubs in patches of sunlight. Here, while walking one day with Alice, I kissed her on the mouth and she let me, and our kissing continued for a long, sweet, seemingly endless moment. Then she said, 'Don't do that. Ever again.'

A grey wolf crossed our path some way ahead, emerging on one side from the brambled undergrowth, delicately negotiating a puddle. 'Look, there's a wolf,' I said, pointing. 'Quick, look – you can still see its tail. Oh, it's gone . . . '

Soon after that day, Alice acquired a boyfriend called R. He owned an antique shop in Islington. She had some doubts about his intelligence. Alice placed 'intelligence' high on her list of priorities for a boyfriend. She was choosing the father of her child as well as her own life partner. I've never known anyone so serious as Alice about choices, about life. A childless woman approaching forty, she felt responsibilities towards herself. I was twenty-nine and terminally indecisive – devoured by longings, by sexual hunger, by romantic dreams. After Alice found R, I got no more kisses from her. A man, however unsatisfactory, was what she wanted. Not a woman.

This was a lonely time. I used to sit in the cemetery and watch the wolves. Sometimes I talked out loud to them. Their faces looked so intelligent, I was sure they understood me. I fed them with bread and biscuits and cake. They liked Mr Kipling's best.

I knew there was something strange about R. Alice

never suspected – which just shows how unreliable sex is as the touchstone of anyone's nature. Contrary to popular lore and fairy stories, we preserve our disguises even in bed. Especially men do, because they seldom have souls, true selves to be revealed. I uncovered R's secret while exploring my own fearful desires. When I was a little girl I had nightmares about wolves, of being eaten by a wolf.

The wolfskin

There was a woman, she lived around here, a long time ago. She had no husband, no pretty little children, no lover, no dear friends, not even a dog or a cat, nothing. She fancied a man, but he was married to someone else. So the woman went to visit her great-aunt, her only living relation, who was a witch. She lived in Somerleyton, in Suffolk, with some other witches, in a witch community.

'Tell me, Great-aunt, how to ensnare the man I love.'

'Puf!' replied the old woman. 'Take my advice and leave him alone. He'll be a pain in the arse and a grief to your heart.'

But the woman persisted. 'I must have this man.'

Grumbling and mumbling her toothless jaws, the old woman went to the chest where she kept all her magic things, including the skins and mummified paws of many different animals. She gave the woman a wolfskin. 'At the full moon, put on this wolfskin. The man will fall in love with you, against his will and good judgement, he will not reject your advances, he will sleep with you and give you a child.'

The woman took the wolfskin and went back home. She waited until the full moon. Then she put on the wolfskin. Except for her breasts, her belly and the parts below, she looked just like a wolf. Even her nails grew into sharp

83

wolf claws and her eyes had a green wolfish glint. She broke into the man's house through a downstairs window. His old mother and father were sleeping on a bench by the fireplace. The wolf-woman killed them both, she ate their flesh, she drank their blood, she crunched up their bones. Then she crept upstairs. In the first bedroom she found a baby and a small child. She ate the baby. The small child woke up. She ate the small child. In the next bedroom, she found the man, lying asleep with his wife beside him. She ate the wife and she lay down beside the man. 'Wake up, dear husband,' she whispered. 'I am ready for you now. Come into me, fill me.'

The man woke, they made love. It was dark in the room. 'Dear wife, how fierce you are tonight. What sharp teeth you have. Draw back the shutters and let me see you. As we are married, we need not be ashamed or fearful of our nakedness.'

'No, husband, I prefer to make love in the dark.'

After a bit the man fell asleep and snored. The wolf-woman lay awake, feeling hungry and disappointed. 'He was not worth it,' she said to herself. 'Next time, I shall find myself a real wolf.'

R's antique shop, the Gothic Castle, is situated just off Upper Street, in a dingy narrow side road. He specializes in Victorian birdcages and fish tanks. Also dusty plastic flowers arranged in cracked vases, stuffed pheasants and mousetraps.

He could never remember my name. Or did he deliberately forget? He disliked most of Alice's friends and acquaintances, all those pre-dating their relationship. He felt 'threatened', as she explained, 'judged' by us. It's true that I thought him a stupid nerd, undeserving of anyone so special and clever as Alice. But that was before I grew suspicious.

Chopin's Nocturnes were playing scratchily on one of those 1920s gramophone players with a silver tube for a record arm. R was slumped in an armchair by the till, reading the *Islington Gazette*. 'Sorry, closed,' he said, not looking up.

'It's Frances,' I said loudly. 'Alice's friend.'

'Oh, er yes.' He blinked at me, through rimless spectacles. He was wearing a striped knitted tanktop over an unbuttoned and torn shirt. 'Can I—?'

'You're a werewolf,' I said. 'Don't trouble to deny it.' I took a gun out of my bag and pointed it at him. It was plastic, but looked convincing. My hands were shaking.

'Don't shoot,' he said, faintly ironic.

Soon after, rummaging in the secondhand bookshop below Vortex Café in Stoke Newington Church Street, I found a book I had given Alice, with both our names written on the flyleaf, scored out.

I didn't just lose Alice, I lost all my friends. I lost them one after the other, with careful violent intention. Like shooting pigeons out of the sky. I said the worst things I'd ever thought of saying. I wrote poisonous letters. I laughed a lot, for no apparent reason. I was sacked from my job. I offended even distant acquaintances and passers-by. I beat a man up in the tube, on the Piccadilly line between Arnos Grove and Southgate. I stole things from shops. I talked wildly and used foul language. I even made my mother cry.

I had strange and surreal dreams. One night I cut off all my hair and it flew away in the sky, twittering like a flock of starlings. My hair was truly, in real life, falling out. I was happier in my dreams. I was seeing doctors.

They injected me, they loaded me down with heavy anchors for safety. I stopped feeling anything. My body went numb, especially my hands and arms and in a circle around my mouth. My eyes itched, they were bleeding poison.

The problem was, I let too much power flood into me at once. You see, I didn't realize, women are different from men. We don't split so easily and cleanly down the middle at will. We turn into whole, real monsters. The wolf entered me, I became the wolf.

In the wasteland, in litter-strewn, desolate streets, past McDonalds, around Dalston Junction, through Ridley Road Market walks the lone and hungry wolf. Oh She-wolf, divine Wolf-bitch, Mother of Wolves, Lupa, transform your votaries into your likeness. By the new moon, under the full moon, in the moon's changes we arise and howl (*collective howl*). Your red-hooded girls, your sweet-fleshed victims, we call on you, oh Mother (*howl repeated*).

(Part of an ancient charm, updated for present-day use, to be spoken by women wishing to invoke the Moon goddess and become werewolves)

Softly and with uncanny grace, his eyes fixed unwaveringly upon me, he moved towards me through the overcrowded empty shop. As the wolf approaches the flock, his prey. I was frozen, hypnotized, by his steady gaze. In those brief moments I regretted not having made a will, as my mother had advised me. I also thought of my unborn children and the novels lost to posterity.

'Please,' he said, stretching out his hand. 'Give me the gun.'

'Stay where you are!' I shouted.

He stopped in front of me. There was a powerful smell

of wolf – a hot sharp stink. Sex or fear. Coming from one of us. He was still in human form, but I feared at any second he might turn.

He touched my face. Where his finger touched, it left a numb spot. 'I'm just a man,' he said, 'like any other man. Normal. And fairly harmless.'

I let the gun drop. I wanted his tongue inside my mouth. 'You're an interesting kind of girl,' he said. 'You hold a lot back, don't you?'

Poison

Wendy Wallace

Rachel moved methodically around the balcony, watering a collection of limp plants in earthenware pots. Their once succulent leaves were shrivelled like the skin of old oranges and the earth had formed a hard crust which repelled the water she poured from a blue plastic jug. It spilled over the edges of the pots and onto the dusty tiles. Rachel enjoyed the nightly ritual of the watering. Her plants were proof of her ability to sustain life in the desert, theirs and hers. She only intended staying for a year or two, so she didn't demand luxuriant growth from them, simply that they shouldn't die.

The flat was at a crossroads, over a butcher's shop. The smell of raw meat lingered on the stairs, along with a gang of scuttling rats that had eaten holes through the wooden partition separating the shop from the stairs to the flat. The rats were dark and quick, and at night, after they had had their fill of the scraps of yellow fat which the butcher let fall to the floor and the single, scaly chickens' feet which, as his religious duty, he piled in a corner for the refugees to take away for soup, then they would make their way to Rachel's kitchen.

Rachel considered the flat ideal. It was cheap and she liked being in the heart of things, as she put it, when her friends commented on the smell on the stairs or the lack of air-conditioning. 'No one,' they said, wiping their upper lips with wads of folded tissues, 'can live without air-conditioning.'

She and Rakhia laughed about that, when Rachel reported these conversations. And Rakhia waved her slim brown hands in the air, the light gold bracelet slipping up her right arm, and said, 'Rachel, my friend. *We* can live without it but perhaps you cannot. I will try my best for you, for another place, a better place.'

'I don't want another place,' Rachel would insist. 'You found me the best place. I'm happy here.' And she meant it.

The thought of Rakhia made her smile. The help she insisted on giving was important but it was her friendship that Rachel valued more, which gave her a way into the life of the country, showed her that she wasn't a prisoner of her own culture, that nobody was – didn't have to be, anyway. Rakhia was her key to the country.

Rachel sloshed the last of the water over a drooping jade plant and stood for a moment looking down on the deserted streets. It was late afternoon and the souk was dead, still in the grip of the afternoon torpor which slowed the whole city between the hours of three and six. At home people slept on floors, finding them cooler than beds; at the airport planes sat paralysed on the melting runway and on the streets even the goats folded their dainty legs under their swollen bellies and rested.

She noticed, for the second time that day, a man squatting on his haunches in the doorway across the narrow street from her flat. He sat perfectly still, his eyes open but unfocussed, as if he were in hibernation. He had a faded shawl drawn over his head and swathed around his neck, falling onto the shoulders of a dirty white djellaba.

A pair of cream-coloured leather shoes, slip-ons with gold
chains across the front, emerged from the hem of the djellaba. As she watched he drew a box of matches and a
single cigarette out of his pocket. The matches were cheap.
Two broke as he struck them and the head of the third
flew off, alight, a small meteorite landing in the dust at
his feet. The fourth match caught and the man raised his
head and looked directly at Rachel, breathing out a drift
of smoke. As she turned to go in she caught a glimpse
of a pointed face, covered in dark stubble, and a pair of
disconcertingly widely-spaced eyes.

She slipped in through the french door to her room and
shut it behind her. The man had been there for nearly four
hours, at least since she came home from the university.
She wished he hadn't caught her eye like that. Something
about him made her uneasy, something more than just his
presence. She shrugged off the thought. People did sit in
doorways, for long periods; there was nothing unusual in
it.

She picked up the receiver of a heavy black telephone
which stood on the desk and dialled Hashim's number,
frowning with the effort of recognizing the Arabic
numerals and of turning the dial, which was stiff.

'*Quaissa?*' he said softly when he heard her voice. They
only ever spoke Arabic to each other on first meeting,
exchanging greetings, and in bed, when he liked to speak
to her in his language and she liked not to understand.

'*Hamdulillah*,' she replied, embarrassed. It was imposs-
ible to speak the language without invoking God, but it
made her feel fraudulent when she did. 'God's just a swear
word to me,' she had joked to Hashim, and she had been
relieved when he laughed.

'Were you still asleep? I felt like talking.'

It was a formality. Hashim would never admit that she

91

had disturbed him. 'No, I am working,' he said. 'It is too hot for sleep.'

'Will I see you tonight?'

'Yes, *habibi*. But late. There is someone I must see.'

They didn't say much on the phone. Nobody did, by that time. There was always a feeling that someone might be listening, although the expatriates Rachel knew scorned the idea. 'You can't even telephone across the river. How could they ever organize phone-tapping? It's a joke.' But Hashim didn't think it was a joke, nor did Rakhia, although she didn't like to talk about security; too proud perhaps, or too afraid?

Really the only safe place to talk was outside, on a patch of clear ground, where you could see for sure whether there was anyone in earshot. Taxis weren't safe, nor were cafés. Offices weren't safe and even in people's houses there was a feeling – that someone who should not be might be listening. Two people out of five, it was said, worked for security. The figure was exaggerated of course. But a lot of people did do it, part-time, passing on a piece of information here, an address there.

'Small-time informants.' Hashim said it with disgust. 'They have turned us into a nation of betrayers.'

Rachel found this a harsh judgement. 'Hmmm,' she would reply. 'But salaries are so low . . . I mean I know it's wrong, but people have to live.'

And Hashim would spit with precision at the ground. 'No, Rachel. We never had salaries here. But once we had dignity.' Hashim was uncompromising. It was part of his charm for Rachel, who found it too easy to see both sides of any question, who always wanted to believe the best of people.

'All right,' she said. 'I'll see you later. Oh Hashim . . . ' But he had gone. She had meant to tell him about the

man. She knew what it was now that bothered her about
him: it was his shoes. They belonged with a safari suit,
not an old djellaba. Hardly conclusive though. She
unbuckled her sandals, lay down on the bed and closed her
eyes.

A mile away, by the river, mosquitoes were congregating
over the head of a young man. He took off his torn shirt,
and half-mast trousers, and folded them carefully, balancing them on a rock a little way from the edge of the water.
Carrying a square of soap in one hand he waded naked
into the river, up to his waist, splashed water over himself,
and began lathering his chest. On the other side of the
road, outside the Palace Hotel, a group of taxi drivers
sprawled in each others' front seats, smoking and talking,
waiting for their customers to emerge for the evening.

The river road had been built in colonial days, and had
received scant attention in the thirty years since Indepen-
dence. It was pitted with holes of varying depth which
drivers were in the habit of swerving to avoid. In one spot
the road was half-barred. A tree had fallen the previous
year and the Ministry of Road, Rail and River Transport
remained in dispute with the Ministry of Public Works
over whose responsibility it was to remove it. The neem
trees which lined the river road were by this time massive-
trunked and taller and more permanent-seeming than any
of the buildings along the river's edge. They lent grace to
the wide pavement which ran between the road and the
river, and cast their shade even-handedly over the naked
bathers and the expensively clad politicians, businessmen
and foreigners who were in the habit of congregating on
the spacious terrace of the Palace Hotel.

The man in the river had finished his chest and was
standing awkwardly on one leg soaping the foot of the

other when a white Mercedes, its windows tinted violet, sped up to the front entrance of the hotel and braked sharply. Two men in safari suits jumped out of the back of the car and strode up the terrace steps, calling to the waiters to fetch the manager.

The man in the river stopped and stared. Their behaviour suggested that the men were from state security, and the number plates on the Mercedes confirmed it. The taxi drivers fell silent and sat up straight. The manager rushed out of the foyer. Without his customary bowtie he looked naked. He darted ahead of the men to the bar at the back of the terrace and stood with his back to the array of imported spirits and liqueurs, his arms spread out protectively.

'In the name of God,' he shouted, his voice shrill and raised. 'Why here? Why here first?'

The smaller of the two men smiled. 'It is the new law. Didn't you know? Give me the storeroom key.' As the manager hesitated, the security man reached for a bottle of crème de menthe, held it up in the air, and dropped it, slowly and deliberately, onto the floor between them.

'God is merciful,' muttered the manager, as the glass splintered on the tiles and the sticky green liquid splashed over his sandalled feet. Soldiers, young men with open faces and black boots, began flooding up the steps onto the terrace.

The bather watched as the soldiers stacked crates of bottled beer on the flat-bed trucks they had arrived in. When the trucks were piled precariously high, they began throwing the crates into the river. An amazed smile spread over the man's face and he ducked down, leaving only his nose and eyes above the swirling brown waters of the river. He stayed there for a long time, watching.

94

Finally the lorries swayed off down the road, the soldiers half-running, half-walking in a column behind them.

The man came out of the water with two armfuls of small green bottles, the square of soap balanced on top. 'The river runs with beer,' he called out, when he reached the shore. 'God is great!' And he threw his head back and began to laugh. He laughed long and loud.

Rachel poured herself some water from a tall glass bottle standing on the table by the bed. She took a mouthful and grimaced. It was warm as bathwater. She drank half the glass and lay down again. It was ridiculous, but watering the plants had almost become an act of defiance. Because on the front balcony of the flat she could be seen from the street. And since the imposition of religious law two months earlier, Rachel had begun to feel that her very existence was an offence. Unveiled, unmarried, female, white. Hers was a set of circumstances for which there was no provision in the ancient laws, designed to rule the existence of women who moved from their fathers' houses to their husbands' at an early age, in a few short steps. It wasn't even as if the Muslims respected the laws themselves.

Everyone said they were just being used as a trick, a way to keep one man in power and the rest down. 'This is not Islam,' they said, strictly in private.

She lay on the bed in the gathering darkness and imagined the charge: watering plants, on a balcony; an incitement to lust. Fifty lashes. She giggled and lit a cigarette then started to cry. The tears rolled sideways down her face and into her ears and she wiped her eyes with her wrist.

Really, Rakhia was in the only possible situation. Being married, and the mother of sons, meant she had status as

a woman, had been through the rites of passage. But she
was divorced, and living with her family, so she was free,
not a slave to childbearing and the charcoal stove. Rachel
loved to visit Rakhia at her mother's house, in the afternoons, after Rakhia had locked the door at the estate
agent's office where she worked as a secretary. She was
called a secretary but as far as Rachel could see she did
all the work; talking on the telephone, charming clients,
soothing landlords. She was always on the phone to someone or other.

Rachel liked nothing better than to go home with
Rakhia for the afternoon, to be taken into the bedroom
Rakhia shared with her two sisters, to lie companionably
head to toe on one of the wooden beds, dressed in a bor-
rowed cotton shift, and listen to their talk, which centred
mainly on 'the business of being a woman,' as Rakhia
called it. 'You know, Rachel. This business of being a
woman. We are suffering by it. In our circumcision, on our
wedding night, when we bring our children to the world.
To be a woman is the same thing as to suffer.'

Rachel would listen with a mixture of fascination and
alarm, eating sugared almonds one after the other because
it didn't seem right to smoke in the bedroom, where magazine pictures of blonde Lebanese women looked disdain-
fully down from the walls at the beaten mud floor and
the glassless windows. Smoking was what men did. And
Rachel, in the company of Rakhia and her sisters, felt
herself sometimes to be more like a man, a man or a large
female child. Certainly she was not a woman as they were.
And she alternated between wanting to be, wanting to
have a body as innocent of hair as a plucked chicken, to
be oiled and perfumed and owned, and revulsion for the
whole thing.

So she let Rakhia dab perfume on her but refused her

offers to pull the hair out of her legs and arms with a ball of sugar glue. She didn't even really enjoy the perfume. Rachel liked the traditional scents, made of fragrant wood brought in from the savanna lands on the backs of camels, the kind Rakhia's mother wore. But Rakhia and her sisters favoured imported concoctions. Poison was Rakhia's favourite. A smug, opaque purple bottle of it stood on her shelf of the cabinet and when Rakhia entered a room the heavy unsettling smell of Poison preceded her and lingered after she had left.

Rachel had stopped talking to Rakhia about Hashim. She had a feeling that she disapproved. Rakhia was keen on romance but not sex. She thought of sex as a dark business, best kept within the confines of marriage. She read a lot of Barbara Cartland, and when Rachel tried to show her there were other things to read, and gave her Beryl Bainbridge and Erica Jong and, as an afterthought, Nawal El Saadawi, she had returned them without comment as if they had been some kind of insult. And when Rakhia had come round unexpectedly one afternoon and found Rachel in her djellaba and Hashim having a shower she had thrown her tea down her throat and almost run out of the door. They hadn't seen each other for a week or two after that, but it had been Rakhia who had telephoned and suggested Friday breakfast. Rachel had accepted with pleasure.

Rakhia thought that Rachel should marry Hashim, even though she didn't really seem to like him. 'If you love the man, Rachel,' she would say, gravely. 'If you have reached this stage where you love the man. You should marry him. So no harm can befall you.'

And Rachel would smile and say, 'We are just friends,' and change the subject. She loved the man, yes, but mar-

riage took more than love. It meant marriage to the
country, because Hashim would never leave.

'How could I?' he would say, sadly, rubbing tired eyes
with thin fingers. 'How could I when things are as they
are?' And he would not expect an answer because there
was none.

Rachel got off the bed and walked into the kitchen,
clapping her hands in front of her to warn the rats of her
arrival. In the darkness the rats were comfortable. They
sipped at water from dishes she left soaking in the sink or
gnawed on candles she kept at strategic spots for use in
power cuts. They pushed at storage tins with their noses
until one fell off a shelf, clattering and frightening them
momentarily back into hiding. Then, emboldened, they
pranced out again to nibble on rice, or Earl Grey tea or
typewriter ribbons. She turned on the light and as she
filled the kettle the call to evening prayers crackled out
over a cheap public address system, distorted and ugly-
sounding as the religion itself had been distorted and made
ugly by the state.

'So no harm can befall me,' she said out loud and sighed.
She knew what Rakhia meant. Under the new laws it was
forbidden for a man and a woman who were not married
or close blood relatives to be alone together. When Rachel
went to see her professor at the university he would osten-
tatiously prop his office door open, as if to prove to
passersby that they were indeed discussing her disser-
tation on Coptic art, and not screwing on the desk. It was
embarrassing. It forced her to wonder what it would be
like to go to bed with him, although before the idea had
never occurred to her. Now you had to think about sex
with every man you met. The law forced you to.

Hashim still came to the flat, discreetly, arriving by taxi
so he wouldn't have to leave his car parked outside, getting

dropped a little distance away. He only came at night now, late, when the souk had quietened, then slipped out in the early hours, leaving her to wake up alone in the wide rope bed.

Still she was afraid. Worse than afraid, guilty. As if their relationship really was something to be ashamed of. She tried to rationalize the guilt away but she couldn't. The laws had seeped into her heart, eroded her sense of who she was, left her with the certainty only of where she was. It was depressing. It would have been unimaginable a few short months ago, when she had arrived in the country, that she could have felt like this. And it was ironic. Because her relationship with Hashim was the purest she had ever had. It was tender and passionate, they understood each other, were kind to each other, and true. And they both knew the limits of it.

She dropped a spoonful of tea into the aluminium kettle on the gas ring, added a fresh mint leaf and left it boiling gently. She came out of the kitchen and onto the back balcony and walked slowly round to the front, breathing in the night air, heavy with the mingled smells of jet fuel and mutton roasting on coals. When she reached the front she glanced down on the street. The man was still there. She walked slowly back again and into her room, her skin prickling with unease.

Rakhia sat at her desk, resting her elbows on its pitted tin surface and running her hands through her hair. Above her head a neon tube was slung from the ceiling with a stiff tangle of wiring. It hummed and stuttered, throwing a cold white light unsteadily over the office.

'Musa,' she called. A young man in shorts and flipflops appeared in the doorway and stood without speaking, his eyes on the floor.

99

'Tea,' she said quietly.

'What?'

'Tea. Bring me tea.' She was almost shouting. 'Are you really so stupid or do you do it to annoy me?' He had gone. 'Poor fool,' she said. 'I think you really are stupid. I should take your salary and make my own tea. Perhaps I will.' No matter how much she worked, how many hours overtime she did, the money was never enough.

She rolled a piece of paper into a gigantic typewriter which sat on the desk and began beating out a letter: 'Dear sirs, We are pleased to inform you we have found a residence for your employee, Mr . . . ' She rummaged in a pile of scruffy papers for the name. McMinter. 'Dear God,' she murmured. 'The names of these people! Every one of them has a different name. Every last one of them. And none of these names means anything.' Rachel's name meant something. 'Oh she was someone's daughter, someone in the Bible,' Rachel had told her, adding hurriedly, 'but that's not why I'm called it. I mean we're not religious or anything. It's just that it was in fashion then . . . '

Rakhia sighed. Rachel. She had tried to tell her, she had tried to explain about the way things were in this country. But Rachel didn't seem to understand. She seemed to think nothing applied to her: the suffering of women; God's laws; the need to marry, not have sex in the afternoons like a dog. Rachel didn't appear to understand anything. And the man she had chosen! Hashim! Who told lies to the world, writing to the BBC that people were being tortured, that the president was a madman. Bringing shame on the country, as if it weren't a mother and father to him, as if it hadn't given him life. Poor Rachel. And yet she liked her in a way. Despite everything, she liked her.

She finished the letter and pulled it out of the machine. The 'p's and 'i's had punched right through the flimsy paper. The letter looked as if it had been sprayed with birdshot. She signed her name neatly at the bottom of it, picked up the telephone and dialled Rachel's number. '*Ya* Rachel. You were resting? Good. How is everything?' She said it as a four-syllable word, ev-ér-y-thing. 'You have heard the news I suppose? I could come to you this evening. Oh is he? How late? Okay. *Ma'salamah.*'

She put down the phone abruptly. Really, this Hashim was too bad. He respected nothing, neither God nor the president, God save him. Certainly he did not respect Rachel; if he did he would not treat her in this way. Poor, foolish Rachel. The man used her as a prostitute. Her face coloured with shame and anger at the idea.

When Musa returned Rakhia was sorting through a pile of keys, each with an addressed paper label tied to it. The keys were large and rusty, old-fashioned keys for old-fashioned locks. She selected one and held it in the palm of her hand for a moment.

'Thank you, Musa,' she said kindly. She slid the key into her soft synthetic leather handbag and left the office without drinking the tea.

It was late by the time Hashim arrived at Rachel's door. Most of the little shops in the souk had closed for the night and the silent streets were being claimed by their night-time occupants: thin dogs running in packs, their howls echoing off the padlocked metal shutters of the shops. At the corner a group of street boys were crouched round a small yellow fire, talking in whispers. One sat a little distance from the others, sucking his thumb and staring at the flames.

Hashim pressed as lightly as it was possible to touch the bell and still make it ring. Rachel, upstairs, was listening for it. She flew down the stairs in the darkness, taking the rats by surprise. One of them dived under the door to the bathroom and got stuck there, its back paws scrabbling uselessly on the smooth stone tiles, its fleshy-looking bottom raised in the air.

She opened the tin door slightly, hiding herself behind it, and she and Hashim went up the stairs and along the balcony in silence, Rachel glancing down to the street as they went. He was still there. The white djellaba reflected the moonlight in a dull sideways gleam. He appeared to be asleep on the ground.

Hashim smelled of soap and clean clothes. In the safety of the room, Rachel put her arms around him and rubbed her face against his. She was half a head taller than he was. 'So?' he had said when she remarked on it. 'We're the odd couple. I like it that way.'

He sat down in her only armchair and tipped his head back against the top of the cushion. 'How are you, my friend?'

'Hashim.'

He raised his head and looked at her.

'There's a man outside. He's been there all day.'

'Hmmm,' he said. 'Is there? Have you heard about the alcohol ban? I think we should have a drink. Celebrate.' He stood up, took a bottle of Johnnie Walker out of the wardrobe and poured two small glasses to the brim with whisky.

'Cheers,' he said, holding one glass out to Rachel and, when she didn't take it, chinking the two glasses together himself.

'For God's sake,' Rachel said. 'Aren't you going to say anything?'

He sighed and put the glasses down on a low table between them. 'Look. I know there is a man outside. I saw the fellow, of course. He is watching. Or perhaps he is not watching. But if he isn't someone else is. Rachel, darling . . . ' He rubbed his eyes with his fingertips. 'You cannot live in this place and be invisible. None of us can. It is necessary to have courage.'

Rachel picked up her glass and turned it slowly round in her hands. 'I know,' she said, eventually. 'But I'm scared. It's as if we're never alone together. There's nowhere to go. I can't relax any more.'

'*Habibi.*' He stroked her face between his two hands. 'Everyone feels that. But these people,' he gestured towards the balcony, 'live out there. They don't live in your head. You mustn't let them. We are all afraid. But better times will come. Nobody is with the government. Only those who are cowed by them may appear to be with them. And meanwhile . . . ' He shrugged and raised his glass. 'Courage.'

They finished the bottle, and ate a newspaper cone of felafel which Hashim produced out of his pocket. 'Never travel without food,' he said. They both knew that they weren't going to go to bed. At midnight, Hashim left.

'Won't it be risky?' Rachel said, at the door.

'Haven't you heard? The river runs with beer. The whole city will be drunk tonight.'

From the balcony, Rachel watched Hashim grow smaller as he walked down the street. The man in the doorway was awake. She could see the tip of his cigarette glowing in the darkness. At the crossroads, Hashim turned suddenly and blew a kiss and Rachel laughed quietly and waved back in defiance. Then she hurried into her room and locked the door.

Rachel dreamed that she was in a prison. The space was so small that she couldn't move in any direction. She could see the ceiling above her, just out of reach, painted with

103

every colour in the world, but she couldn't find the walls. As she peered around, someone outside began banging on the door. The banging went on and on, the hollow vibration of knuckles beating on tin.

'I can't see the door,' she called out, trying to make herself heard above the noise. 'I can't open it. I don't know where it is!'

She woke up as the banging stopped and a key shot back the lock in the door downstairs. For a moment she didn't move, but lay straining her ears for something which would tell her that it was another gate, or part of her dream. Then she heard men's voices approaching up the stairs and almost fell out of bed, her heart pounding so fast and hard she thought she might be dying.

'Who is it?' she shouted, in a voice high with terror. 'What do you want?' There was a pause.

'Rachel?' said a voice, speaking in intimate tones on the other side of the door. 'Open please. It is police.'

'Bobbies,' said another voice, and there was laughter.

'Wait.' She found her jeans and pulled them on, banging her forehead on the wardrobe door as she bent forwards. She put on a sweatshirt and turned on the light. 'I am opening the door,' she said unsteadily.

She unbolted half of the french doors and stepped back into the centre of the room as they crowded through the narrow entrance. They looked so much like the stereotype of themselves she almost smiled. 'Brutes in suits' Hashim had called the security forces in a piece for *Middle East World*. And here they were, four of them, crammed into dirty, ill-fitting, cream-coloured suits, staring with naked interest at her and her room.

'So, Rachel,' said the one in front, putting out his hand and stepping towards her. 'How do you do?' He said it as a question. The smell of alcohol came off him so strongly it was almost tangible.

She locked her hands behind her back and looked at the ceiling.

'Where is your – what shall we call him? – your friend?'

She looked at him again. 'What friend?' For a moment she thought he meant Rakhia. 'What friend?'

'Rachel. There is no need for this. I am asking you the whereabouts of Mr Hashim.'

She looked at him in astonishment. 'I don't know. He's not here.' Your man watched him go, she wanted to say. Didn't he tell you? Weren't the phones working?

The blood rose into the man's face. He hissed something over his shoulder and the other men left the room reluctantly, tiptoeing with exaggerated care around the small table with the empty glasses still on it. She heard the kitchen door grind over the tiles and simultaneously the sound of splintering wood from the balcony.

The man looked her up and down with contempt. 'Where is Hashim?' he said, slowly.

She felt suddenly triumphant. She smiled. 'I don't know. And if I did, I wouldn't . . . '

His hand flew out and he punched her between the legs. She gasped and fell backwards into the armchair. 'Dirty bitch,' he said in Arabic. 'Dirty white meat.' And he followed the others out of the room.

Rachel stayed in the armchair and stared at the floor. She looked at the tiny chips of glittering stone set into the grey slate. She noticed disinterestedly the way the dust had settled in narrow channels in the grooves between the tiles. She got up calmly and opened the desk drawer, reaching into the back of it for her passport and her remaining travellers cheques in their cumbersome plastic wallet. Passport, money, tickets, keys. She went through

her litany of departure. Well, she didn't have a ticket. She
hadn't planned on going anywhere. She felt in the bottom
of her bag. She had the key. How had they got in? How
the hell had they got in?

The men walked two in front and two behind as they
escorted Rachel along the balcony. She looked at her
plants. In the pre-dawn light they looked unfamiliar. They
were a poor collection, she realized suddenly, transplanted
onto a ledge in the sun in their constraining little pots.
They would die without her. They were half-dead already.
The five of them trod along the balcony and down the
steps.

The door to the street hung open on its hinges. One of
the men held a car door open and Rachel climbed in,
clutching her bag on her lap. He slammed the door shut
and she closed her eyes and breathed in long and hard.
There was a sweet, heavy smell in the car. She opened
her eyes and breathed in again. It was oppressive. It was
unmistakable. She pressed her forehead against the cold
glass in the car window and stared out, seeing only
Rakhia's smiling face.

It was cold on the street. A wind had sprung up from
nowhere, the way it can do at night in the desert. The man
in the doorway shivered and woke up in time to see a car
pulling away from the butcher's shop. As the car passed
him a foreign woman's face looked out at him, pale as
the moon. She seemed to be crying. She looked vaguely
familiar. He drew his shawl tighter around his shoulders
as the car drew away down the deserted street.

'God protect her,' he muttered to himself. 'God protect
all of us.' In the distance the call to morning prayers
sounded, bleak and lonely, as if God himself were answer-
ing out of the night.

Night Shifts

Andie Hawthorn

It's getting bad. I've been dreaming about you again. I'm underwater, looking up at you, trying to surface, but every time I try, your hand reaches out as though to stroke me and pushes me under. My feet don't touch the bottom. I wake up gasping like a fish, in a shock of orgasm, like falling through the sky without a parachute. Catch me. I'm falling off the edge. Compared to yours, my own hands are alien.

Schizophrenic Diana says I am a Martian with psychopathic tendencies. I smile at her through the glass walls of the nurses' station and write, '11.45 pm. Diana seems wakeful tonight.' She presses her nose against the glass and tries to read what I have written. I hold the page up for her to see and she creases up with laughter. She thinks I am her friend because I don't chivvy her into occupational therapy or ward meetings. I give her sedatives and warm drinks. We have a laugh. She thinks we look related because we both have uneven front teeth and dark circles around our eyes. I open the door.

'What is it, Diana? Don't you want to sleep?'

She stops laughing and stares at me. 'I've got my Depixol injection tomorrow.'

'I know.'

On day shift I once helped to hold Diana down for her injection which she always refused. It took five of us, four to hold her and one to administer the injection. She can't refuse the treatment because she is under section. She struggled for a while, then her body went limp and she cried, 'Mama, Mama,' just like a doll when you tip it backwards.

I stroked her head and said, 'You'll be all right, you'll be all right.' After the injection she looked at me, her eyes wet and helpless, like a lover after fucking.

I want to melt you down and inject you warm into my veins.

I am still a junkie at heart. I had a rich father, neat bookshelves made of stripped pine filled with assorted classics and pot plants hanging from macramé holders, which confused you. You didn't think I was the type. I never let you watch me because it was private, even from you. You wouldn't understand. No, I was not ashamed. I gave it up for you and it was nothing, nothing at all, compared to losing you. Believe me: cold turkey is easy in the right environment, no worse than a few days of bad flu.

You held my head in your lap and said, 'You'll be all right, you'll be all right,' and my eyes opened and fixed on you. Heroin is safe if you have a good source, regular meals and keep a clean needle. Love is dangerous.

Charge Nurse Alvin has been pilfering amphetamines again. It's an open secret. It's easier on night shift when there is less work. On a good night all we have to do is hand out drinks and medication, then go around every hour making sure everyone is still there and alive.

I have been playing draughts in the TV lounge with Diana who can't sleep, not surprising since she hides the capsules under her tongue and spits them out when she thinks no one is looking. She is wearing her Rochester's Mad Wife expression.

'Are you God?' she says, 'do you know everything?'

'Yes, everything.'

'Why are they going to force me to have the injection tomorrow?'

'Because you're a schizophrenic.'

Diana laughs, hissing between her teeth, as though I had cracked an obscene joke. Her hair falls in dark ringlets over her face as she nods her head.

'Why am I a schizophrenic?'

'I give up. Why are you?'

'You should know if you're God.'

'Don't ask me. I just wound the universe up and let it go. Do you want some Ovaltine?'

You made me promise never to use again. For you I came out of my white cocoon and you let me go skinless into the world. Love is a terrible thing and I want my habit back. I have made an appointment to see my gentleman doctor in Wigmore Street. He is courteous and discreet and never asks for more than I can give.

Who are you anyway? You are not the person I trusted. Sometimes I think I must have invented you. Is it possible to mourn someone who never really existed? For days at a time I forget what you look like, only the feel of you remains.

The ward is divided up into small dormitories and single rooms. It is ward policy to house like with like so the six girls with anorexia nervosa are all in one dormitory, the mothers with puerperal psychosis in another and so on.

109

Less clubable patients like Diana and Simon the psychopath have single rooms. On a quiet night it is possible to believe that all these sleeping bodies are just corpses in a mortuary waiting for the resurrection.

Diana follows me along the shiny corridor to the small kitchen where I heat some milk on the Baby Belling. In her pink nightdress and bare feet she is small and trusting as a child, yet she is older than I am. She fingers the embroidery on the sleeve of my blouse.

'Why don't you ever wear uniforms here?'

'To help promote an atmosphere of healthy informality.'

Diana peers at me as though trying to read bad subtitles. 'You still look like a nurse.'

'That's interesting. I wonder why.'

Diana caresses the air with graceful twists of her hand. 'I think it must be in the skin.' Her skin is pale and blotchy. She needs vitamins and fresh air. She asks, 'Do you love me?'

'I love everybody. I'm God.' She winces and laughs. It isn't what she wants, this banter.

'Yes, Diana, I love you in my fashion.'

Her back straightens and her eyes grow bright and alert. 'Thank you,' she says with dignity. 'Oh, thank you.' She looks queenly and not mad at all.

I don't know what love is; you said so. There are times when I am sure I must have come close. I remember you on the station platform, holdall in one hand, guitar in the other, ticket between your teeth and looking as though the brick road to heaven was paved wherever you happened to be. Your neck was exposed because you had had all your hair cut off. I cupped my hands around your neck to shield it from the wind and we stood kissing, not caring who looked. That was love, or something like it.

I remember how you cried out after having an orgasm, as though you had lost something. You said, 'This is as far and near as we will ever get and it isn't enough.'

I said, 'What do you want? Whatever it is, you can have it.'

'You don't understand,' you said, 'you haven't suffered enough.'

I wonder now who you thought you were talking to. You never understood about junkies. You thought I needed lessons in how to deal with reality, as though I hadn't made a considered choice. Each to their own poison, I always say. What do you always say? I've forgotten. What do you think about as you look out at the disappearing stars and each grey morning takes you further away from me? What will you say at the end of a lifetime of separating days and nights? How can you bear it?

I hear that you spend your time with the one I nicknamed KGB because she was sent by your friends to spy on us. Her reports were not favourable because she had me marked as a bourgeois individualist who would never fight against the assumptions of my class and culture. She told me so. She grilled me whenever you left the room. I told her that I had no class and very little culture. She wasn't impressed. Someone had done their homework on me. A street junkie she could have tolerated, but not my sort, and in any case she was in love with you. She wore an anorak covered in badges with slogans and clenched fists which she never took off, however warm the room. She sat like a coiled spring and watched me picking away at the fluffballs of your integrity. She visited me one day. We watched Newsnight *together, some poli-*

ticians arguing about the inflation rate and the signifi-
cance of the latest unemployment figures. She wanted to
know what I thought and I told her I didn't think any-
thing, I wasn't interested in party politics.

She said, 'What are you interested in?' and I said 'Sex
and drugs and rock and roll.'

We got drunk together and she told me that one of the
things she loved about you was that you cared deeply
about suffering and injustice. 'We are each other's keep-
ers, like it or not,' she said sternly and I told her the
Russian saying which had amused you so much: 'Olya's
fucking Kolya, Kolya's fucking Solya, and what's it to
you, Tolya?'

It was the only time I ever saw her smile. She said,
'You realize this means war?'

There has been a disturbance. Jane from the mother and
baby unit is in Bathroom Three throwing water over herself and screaming. She is terrified because she thinks that
her body is decomposing. The noise has woken Simon who
is in the corridor in his silk dressing gown saying, 'Tell
her to shut her face or I'll shut it for her, okay?'

Alvin says, 'Cool it, Simon,' but doesn't meet his eyes
which are cobalt blue and crystal with suppressed violence.
Last night he threatened to fracture Alvin's jaw for being
a cheeky black bastard.

'Oh God,' cries Jane, 'I'm rotting alive.' Her baby is
screaming from the cot in the dormitory, Janine and I
are trying to soothe Jane and Simon is clenching and
unclenching his fists.

Diana appears from her room, still sipping Ovaltine. She
smiles sweetly and seductively at Simon and says, 'You
send shivers up my spine, you know that, don't you?'

112

Simon walks back to his room looking pleased and disdainful.

'If your body is starting to rot,' Diana says to Jane, 'the best thing you can do is to rub petroleum jelly on it. It reverses the process.' Jane considers this piece of wisdom and allows herself to be led away by Janine and Alvin. Diana looks at me earnestly. 'Why is Jane decomposing?'

'She isn't, it's a delusion.'

Diana breathes in sharply and begins to cry. 'For God's sake,' she says, 'you'll make her really mad if you tell her that. Can't you feel anything?'

'Diana, you should get some sleep.'

'I will, but promise you won't let them give me the injection?'

'You know I can't.'

She stops crying and looks at me shrewdly. 'Are you in mourning?'

'Yes, I'm God and I'm in mourning.'

'Are we having jokes together?'

'I think so, yes.'

'Good,' she says. 'I need friends. I need your help.' She walks back to her room, alert as a child on Christmas Eve.

Janine paces the floor with Jane's baby who bats her head against Janine's neck looking for a breast.

'You want to fuck around,' said KGB. 'Do your own thing and no price to pay. That's fine, but on whose back?' She was pacing the room in her Doc Martens looking as though she would draw a six-shooter at any moment and hold it to my head. You were in the kitchen practising twelve bar blues and the tin kettle whistled in harmony. The music and the whistling stopped and I knew you were listening. I wanted you to come to me then and fuck me right there on her bed while she watched and

113

*shrivelled up from the heat of it. You stayed in the kitchen
listening for my answer. I could hear you breathing. I
could feel the movement of the blood in your body rising
to your neck and cheeks, picture the moisture glistening
on the curve of your upper lip. Your passivity was frightening me half to death.*

*I should have defended myself. It was what you wanted,
that I should take a stand, that you should know where
to place me. You called me a chameleon and it wasn't a
compliment. It wasn't true either, I never fooled your
friends. I thought it was enough that we should want
each other. I thought it was enough that I was good at
my job.*

*'So are executioners,' said KGB and I blew smoke rings
into your face and said, 'Well somebody's got to do the
job.' She never liked it when anyone else cracked the
funnies. You began to hate my jokes too.*

'We've got an admission,' says Alvin.

Janine wrinkles her nose. 'What, now?'

'She's coming up from casualty,' says Alvin. 'She's been
cutting herself with razor blades. Suicide risk.'

'So why don't they keep her till morning?'

'What do you think? Beds.'

'We haven't got beds to spare either.'

'We've got *one*,' says Alvin.

'What about the referrals we're expecting tomorrow?'

'I dunno,' says Alvin. 'Let the day shift sort it out.' The
muscles are tight around his mouth. He needs coffee and
a cigarette. 'A punter's a punter, what do you want me to
do?'

Janine and I go to the dormitory to prepare the bed,
bantering in whispers to stop ourselves from yawning.

'What's black, white and red?'

'A newspaper.'

'Wrong. A sunburnt penguin.'

'Stop clowning around,' you said. 'Why can't you stop clowning around? I never know where you're coming from. You don't want to see because you don't want to act. You want to anaesthetize yourself so you can feel pure and untouchable.'

I pulled your face close to mine so that our lips touched. You kissed me then, you couldn't help it. Our hearts were open and hungry like the mouths of young birds. You were craving too. You fixed on me, who could never satisfy you.

It is 3.00 am, the witching hour on a night shift, just before you get your second wind, when you count the hours till you can get your head down and wonder what you are doing with your life.

'I'm sick of this,' says Janine. 'I'm going to Jamaica in the summer. See my folks. I'm thinking of leaving Yvette with them. There's no life here for her.' Janine wears a photograph of Yvette hidden inside a silver locket studded with garnets on a chain around her neck.

'Won't you miss her?'

Janine bites her thumbnail and shrugs. 'Child-minder sees more of her than I do. No life.'

The new admission is delivered to us in a wheelchair, reeking of antiseptic. She has cut herself in neat little slashes all over her arms, thighs and face. I look briefly at her notes. She is sixteen years old today and has tried twice to overdose.

Janine says, 'Do you want something to help you sleep?'

'Yes,' she says, falling back onto the pillow, 'yes please. Thank you.' She is nicely spoken, as though she has been brought up to mind her Ps and Qs. 'It's my birthday,' she says and begins sobbing. It is the dry, tearless kind of sobbing that comes from the stomach, the kind you have to watch. I sit by her head with a hand on her shoulder.

'What's on your mind?'

'I can't any more,' she says between sobs. 'I can't do it any more.'

'What can't you do?'

Her sobs become faster.

Janine frowns and shakes her head at me. She says, 'Take these and get some sleep. You'll be all right. You'll be fine.'

The cuts on the girl's face are red and slightly raised, with half an inch between each one. It looks as though she has been through some kind of tribal scarring ritual.

My love, it isn't true. I am not pure, I am adulterated through and through. You have a soul which gleams. You have sharp edges too which shine brightly like new razor blades. 'Feel me,' you said. 'Feel me doing this to you. You don't know you've been born. Open your eyes.' I cut myself on your sharp edges.

'What's the matter?' says Janine. 'You look funny.'

I want who I want and no price to pay, free, and no penalties. I want to twine myself around you like a snake around a tree, feel the green sap rising, bite you to death. Forgive me. I am frantic with wanting.

'Come to think of it,' says Janine, 'you've been looking funny all night.'

'I need a break. I'm fine.'

'I've been reading about people like us,' she says. 'We need constructive feedback and support otherwise we get burnt out.'

116

'Well I never!'

'Yeah. And the cuts.' She makes slashing movements in the air with her hands.

'What about them?'

'More pressure.'

'You don't say?'

'Yeah.' We stand in the white corridor and giggle.

'What's going on?' says Alvin. 'Time to do the rounds. Jane's getting ready to throw another wobbler, Annabel's throwing up in Bathroom Two and Diana's still beefing on about the injection. I've made a note about her medication. Are you sure she swallowed it? She looks high as a kite to me.'

In the TV lounge Simon has tuned in to Capital Radio at full volume. The gibberish sound of a chattering DJ echoes along the corridor. Simon is breaking the rules which state that the radio and television should not be allowed to disturb other patients before 7.00 am. He stands at the threshold with his dressing gown sleeves rolled up to his elbows, cracking his knuckles. He has slicked his hair back with gel. Janine and I chorus, 'Hello, Simon,' and walk past.

Diana is standing at the foot of her bed with her back to me. She is dressed in a long black evening dress with chiffon sleeves. Her hair is carefully piled and pinned at the top of her head and there is a string of pearls around her neck secured at the back with a diamond clasp. She turns to face me. Her skin is pale and shining with layers of ivory foundation cream. Her eyes are heavily made-up in black and grey and her lips are stained a dark plum colour.

'Listen, Diana—'

'Please come in and shut the door behind you.'

I walk to her bed and sit, resting my elbows on my

117

knees. 'Is this just a bit of fun or are you planning on going somewhere?'

'Yes,' she says, 'with your help.'

'Oh dear.'

Her eyes are hawk-like, glittering. The energy coming from her is so strong that my skin begins to prickle. 'Can you feel it?' she asks.

'Listen, Diana, I'm sorry but it's been a long night and I don't think I can handle this.'

'I know. I feel for you, but you must help me to leave here before morning comes. If I'm forced to have another injection I'll go mad. Also, I need a place to stay, to hide for a while.'

'They'll catch you.'

'Perhaps, but I've got no choice. I'm not as helpless as you may think. I need legal advice. I need friends.'

I stand up and pace the floor of her room, cursing and clenching my fists. Diana moves back against the wall as though to give me space.

The feel of you is strong in my body. There are bruises on my thighs, inside my head and around my heart. You have sensitized me. There are particles of pain with sharp edges in the air, we draw them in with each breath, we are all dying on our feet and I can't any more, without a fix, do you understand, keep one foot moving in front of the other, can't do it any more. Listen to me. You are right, I am a double-dealer with a double-dealing soul. I would trade you in this minute, you and your gleaming soul, trade them both for a fix. I want it badly. I want it more than I want you.

'Shit, Diana, why did you let them catch you in the first place? Why didn't you fuck off out of here long ago? Why should anyone pin you down and do disgusting things to

118

your body and mess you about and tell you it's okay? What do you want to be a bloody schizophrenic for?'

'Why are you a drug addict?' she whispers. I am stopped in my tracks.

'Where did you get that idea from?'

'I'm a bit psychic – haven't you noticed? I just know things. It's a problem, actually.' Her eyes begin to shift anxiously from side to side. 'Are you going to help me?'

'No.' But I take a pen from my pocket. She hands me a piece of paper. 'Absolutely not.' I write your name, address and telephone number on the paper, put the pen in my pocket and walk to the door. I look out and see Alvin, Janine and the two auxiliaries through the glass walls of the nurses' station, writing handover notes. Diana takes a black shawl from her cupboard, picks up a patent leather handbag and puts the piece of paper inside it. She slips past me into the white corridor.

'Diana,' I say quietly, 'you look ridiculous.' She is startled.

'Am I beautiful?'

'Yes, very.'

I watch as she glides ghost-like across the corridor on soft leather shoes and lets herself out of the entrance to the ward, heading for the lift.

I know a secret about you; some lines of poetry by Osip Mandelstam you scribbled down in miniature on a crumpled piece of paper that I found in my wastepaper basket:

> *'O where are you, sacred islands,*
> *where no one eats broken bread,*
> *where there is only honey, wine and milk,*
> *creaking labour does not cloud the sky,*
> *and the wheel turns easily?'*

119

Alvin looks up as I enter the nurses' station.
  'All quiet now?'
  'As the grave.'

But Come, I Have Unbosom'd My Soul

Christina Dunhill

The birds are in the garden, I can hear them. The blackbird is singing melodies so complicated it sounds as if he's trying to get the words out. Ten years ago we planted trees to bring the birds in. I know there are bluetits sitting in the trellising out there and hopping low in the hydrangea branches, looking for flies. I'm not used to telling the truth, I confess.

These starting-to-warm days when the light's bright, sex comes seeping in like an old film, the first film you ever saw. I keep the curtains drawn against the thought of skin. Up close to me. The smell of it. The taste of it flickering up through my nose. The little hairs on your skin against my tongue. The slightly bitter taste of you. The memories that go rolling round the mouth, that sit on the palate and coat the teeth. I'd like to spit them out but then I'd be empty. I know this. Seeds and husks in my teeth where love was.

I noticed that you did not age, my darling. Perhaps you didn't really live. Things flowed through you. You were a transmitter; giving off signals and refraining from speech. I wanted to give you all the world there is to give. You soaked up my words and put them away somewhere. You plugged into me for calories and fell back into your coolness. I had known for some time that you were loose. And wet, so wet; I couldn't keep you more than a morning drizzle. Couldn't resist you. You lived in this house like the seasons. Eleven years it would have been this April.

I've incarcerated myself these last few weeks against the coming of spring. I rarely leave my drawing room; I do not leave the house. If I went outside then people would talk. They'd say, 'Look, that woman's wearing her cunt on her sleeve.' Everything comes back to you these days: floating down the river, decked with seaweed, down the big stream to your young love. Damn you.

This is a time to embrace solitude. I will no longer inflict my passions on another and say – as we all say in love – that it's all right. Everything. Everything will be all right. What rubbish, as my friend said of Sita's vow to Rama. I don't want to lose myself again. All love is loss. Sooner or later, even if it's only death. I've no longer the stomach for it.

The business conducts itself well enough from my armchair here. I'm surprised. I always traded so much on personal contact. The boy answers my calls now. People are intrigued. Think I've expanded. 'I've got a secretary,' I say, 'I'm out so much.'

He enters with the telephone on a salver. I relish this. My last days like a Fassbinder movie. 'It's New York,' he says, 'urgent.'

'Tell them I'm away on business,' I reply. 'Tell them to call next week. Cecil,' I say, 'I require absolute discretion from you, that is fifty per cent of your job.' I imagine him gossiping with clients. 'Between you and me . . . '

Between you and me, darling, was a whole world. Sometimes nothing, barely flesh between us. So close, you said, bone-close. You lied. Not one lie. Not even a succession. Everything. Shall I ask the boy for a knife?

122

It is the time of year when you and I started. April, when the japonica blooms, the anniversary of my father's death. Eleven years ago I seduced you in your mother's sitting room, early it was, just before dawn. We looked out of the french windows onto the black outline of an early cherry in bloom as we muscled our way between two sleeping labradors. Or did you seduce me? I remember my fingers in your knickers. Probably just about the time I'm writing this. Thinking of shoots pushing through the ground. Thinking of the man unfleshed. Later that day, I recall, it snowed.

Can you imagine a young man called Cecil? He parts his hair in the centre and seems to have been born in his suit. He slides through the room like a ruler. I've never encountered a human being with so little hip movement. Mince, can't you? I want to say. Mince, damn it. 'Thank you, Cecil,' I say with the broad smile of those with a stake in the world. 'That will be all.'

'Is everything all right, madam?' he says and I wonder if he wants me to talk to him. What is he thinking under his oiled hair and opaque skin? Where does he go when I've dismissed him for the evening? Out to see South London cousins in the bookmaking business? How does he manage on what I pay him? Perhaps he sells his indefinably narrow arse.

Who are his family? I wonder. What parents would consign their son to factotuming for a middle-aged woman in Palmers Green? His vowels are flat and he neglects his terminal consonants. I could teach him elocution. He is certainly inspired by discipline.

This is hell. It is odd to think I have entered hell here in my beautiful drawing room. Perhaps I should call in the *Observer* before I leave: Ursula Fanshawe in 'A Room of Your Own'.

When you lived here we bathed every day in scented oil. We dressed each other's hair. I only wash now when the reek assaults me. My nose is deadened with tobacco. Plugging the Balkan Sobranie into the meerschaum is the one old pleasure that still gives satisfaction; leafing back the crenellated waxen paper, fingering the little plugs and strands out of the tin and pushing them into the bowl. God knows, I drink too, but it blots out the wrong memories.

Your kisses were cold and wet, like running my tongue round the bottom of a pond, but sweet like blancmange. Indescribable. Eleven years and I never got used to it. I'd have to warm you up, sour you down. What do we do about telling the truth? You've absconded with my truth, my darling, and you'll never tell it.

For nothing, for nothing. Who dares whisper it over the gravestones? It's the devil or the deep blue sea. You were the deep blue sea, I guess. The taste of you, like plankton. The look of you, coming up from my thighs with your features blurred. My fingers inside you; it made my head burn; it made me shake. I'm lost in the wild, here in the drawing room, filling my mouth with those fancy cakes Cecil likes to serve. I find them satisfactory. I never liked sweet things. I keep the curtains drawn these days – nets and drapes – and the lights low. After you went, I started to look at women from the window.

Sometimes, I'm afraid, my body aches for it. Some days I cannot stop the heat at the back of my eyes for the need of someone to hold. My arms feel as if their insides have been scooped out. And there are times when my genitals ache. We have worked, I'm told the women in New Guinea say – and if they don't, then somebody should – until our vaginas were hanging out.

I am plotting my suspense novel; gothic figures in capes flit at the edges of this room. I have bought a gas lamp to put the shadows to motion and send them winging. The little pools of light are always you. Frequently the shadows are Cecil. He replaces ashtrays as if he's in training for the Savoy. I wonder occasionally if that boy is the product of a natural birth. There is something decadent about his skin, yet there are no lines on it. I know he wants me to tell him my life story. He thinks I won't last long on memories and fairy cakes. I was never an honest person, but then . . .

'Ms Fanshawe,' he said to me one day, 'I have not wanted to trouble you but think I must. I fear you have a vexatious caller.'

'What on earth do you mean?' I said.

'One or two abortive calls these days are to be expected, madam; the exchanges are overloaded. Wrong numbers occur more frequently now that a gentleman's fingers may be too large for effective push button operation.'

'What *are* you talking about, Cecil?'

'There are too many such calls, madam. I wonder if someone is trying to contact you . . . and cannot bring himself to speak.'

You who have made yourself nothing are calling me, I thought. I will pay you no mind.

'Should I perhaps report the matter to the police?' Polees, he says as if auditioning for a forties play.

'That's quite enough, Cecil,' I said, 'I'm tired.'

What are you doing now, Elean? Are you laughing your deep wide laugh to the back of your throat? Is she captivated? Does she love the way the lines furrow your cheeks then? Does she bury her face in your thick brown hair? Does she sit with her arms round your knees? I saw her, you know: one of those born-again, would-be spring chicks with their hair chopped tight to their scalps and bleached yellow. Walked like a lorry driver. Worked in video, didn't she?

Is she bored with you yet? With your sonnets on the trees and your nocturnes at the piano? Wouldn't she rather be snorting up with her smart friends in Spitalfields? Punching the air to house music? How long can you encage your peculiar canary? As long as I kept you, my darling, my life, here with me? As long would take you to your grave. Would she invite me to your funeral, I wonder? Would she say, eleven years from now: 'Can we be friends? I loved her too. Terribly. I'm afraid it will kill me.'

I've begun to grow tired of the city. This is a whisper. Some mornings I can't think of a reason to get up. I'm wrenching back my last tentacles, and half of them are broken, dear, from limpeting on you. One morning, I woke up like clockwork just before dawn. It seemed as if half the day had passed before Cecil brought the post and my morning roll and coffee. And it was still dark. I could hear the rain crashing down in one of those freak storms which have become a feature of contemporary life. There were feathers on the shoulders of Cecil's jacket. Green, white and pale blue, little tufts like breast feathers.

'I'll have a dry martini,' I said.

The area where his eyebrows should be lifted a fraction. 'Of course, madam.'

When he placed the tray on the sidetable, a lock of hair fell over his forehead and I imagined he was straining not to push it back through his fingers.

'Are you quite happy here, Cecil?'

He straightened his back and capped the bottle. 'Most comfortable.'

'Tell me, do you believe in dreams?'

'In what sense, madam?'

'As auguries, Cecil. It's time that suit went to the cleaners.'

'Of course, Ms Fanshawe. And I am intrigued by the unconscious.'

'Listen carefully, young man, I'd appreciate any help you can give me. Last night I dreamed I was watching a play of the crucifixion. The curtain lifted on the two robbers on their crosses.

' "Oh, you were always a scurvy ruffian!"

' "Never could hold a candle to you! Knave! Your death'll be a service to the world. I'd drive a nail in meself! Be a pleasure."

' "Your hands are tied, dear, remember."

'Then, sure enough, the son of god tramped on, smeared with stage dirt and followed by his entourage.

' "I haven't got all day you know. Just get it up." (Here, Cecil, I am afraid the dying Barabbas pulled a Frankie Howerd expression.)

' "Some of us have meetings tomorrow," continued the son of god. "An impatient man, my father, do you know what he owns?"

'They lashed the trunks together while he stood scratching his bum through his loincloth. He lay on the cross before they were ready and one of the soldiers lunged at him; this was thirsty work, after all. "Can't hurt me, you know," he says. "I'm the almighty. See this blood? You'll be drinking it before breakfast."

'I turned it off, Cecil. It had turned into television and I don't watch melodrama. Hours later it just came back on; it was halfway through the night. The godman stepped down from the cross without a grimace and walked towards me. He took off his loincloth to mop his side.

127

' "Do you want to go to bed with me?" he said.

' "Cover yourself up," I said, "you're a grown man. Women of my age and sexual persuasion do not appreciate this sort of thing."

' "Go on!" he said. "I'm going to die tonight."

' "Sausages!" I said. "I've read the story."

'Well, Cecil, what do you think?'

Something at the side of his mouth flickered. I was seized suddenly with the idea he feared I intended to seduce him.

'I don't know, madam. What happened then?'

'Nothing. That was the end.'

He mumbled something that sounded like, 'It's not a bad sign.'

'What's that?' I said.

'I'm sure I don't know, I don't know at all.'

I started to open the mail. 'No calls till this afternoon, please,' I said.

One day I will hate you and all will be well. Seeds and husks in my teeth where love was. Perhaps one day it will not be like this.

Heaven. Bloody heaven. We always think there will be a replacement. There has to be a replacement. A pace-maker, a new kidney, a hip. A world substitute, another world. We link it to deserts. 'Promoted to glory' – that's what it says on the William Booth memorial. It can't have been for nothing. It can't have been for nothing. For nothing at all.

An invitation arrived in the post. A curious affair, pink and silver with crinkled edges like an old photograph, like a wedding invitation. The pleasure of your company is requested, it said, at an extravaganza by the Masked Players of the Dawn. Something made me take it out of the

128

rubbish bin where I'd first thrown it. I could not help wondering, my darling, if it was an encrypted communication from you. If so, I was not up to it. I tried all my crossword skills to recluster the letters into some kind of message. It exhausted me.

I woke as my head jolted onto my chest and the glass shattered on the side table. It was dark enough for evening but the clock showed only three. Cecil was there in minutes, on his knees, mopping the carpet. My head pounded. I put my hand on his shoulder. 'Forgive me, Cecil. I must lie down.' He took my hand in his cool fingers and put an arm round my waist without touching it with his other hand. A discreet and deferent boy. Where do they breed them? I am a fortunate woman. A deep-seated fear of the female flesh, more like, I remember thinking. I found myself lying on the sofa in underskirt and blouse, propped up on several white pillows.

'I took the liberty of calling the doctor, madam. Can I bring you something? Brandy? A cup of tea?'

'Tea, dear boy,' I said, and was struck again by the notion that he would be logging this in for his tabloid memorial.

A scrawny young woman arrived, wearing too much make-up. 'Dr Bukowski.' She shook my hand before examining me. I didn't know they let doctors wear chipped nail varnish. 'Some stabilizers, rest and a diet, I think, don't you?'

'A diet?' I said. 'Young woman, where have you been for the past fifteen years? I am quite comfortable with my body, I thank you.'

'You will find it stabilizing,' she replied.

'Dr Bukowski, I am familiar with the concept of regular meals.'

'What is the matter, do you think?'

'A disturbance of the psyche, I would say. A confusion of the heart and spirit. All those organs invisible in *Gray's Anatomy*. How do you treat them, Dr Bukowski?'

'With diet and stabilizers, Ms Fanshawe. We target the nearest organ. We prohibit those things which will stop the brain from being flooded with oxygen. We purify the kidneys with grape juice and spring water. We saturate the blood with vitamins. Our aim is to induce pleasure in the condition of life.'

I realized I was staring at her. 'How long have you been with the practice, Dr Bukowski?'

'Six months. I was in Leeds before that. I will call on you again in three days' time. Please rest in bed till then and observe the diet scrupulously. Where is Mr Barrett? Shall I leave the prescription with him?'

I rang for Cecil and let him show her out and go for the prescription. He returned with a large brown bottle containing fat pills like granular slugs. The label gave a Latin name but, as we know, even bindweed has a Latin name. I took two and had to struggle not to vomit. They made me feel quite peculiar.

'Cecil, I don't want to hear a word about this diet until tomorrow, do you understand?'

He nodded.

'Did you tell that idiotic young woman I'd been drinking?'

'No, Ms Fanshawe.'

'Good. I don't sleep with men, Cecil, do you?'

'Madam?'

'I sleep with women, Cecil. Do you?'

'Madam!'

'What do you like doing, eh, boy? Sit down and talk to me, man to man. Fetch me another drink.'

130

He slid out of the room and reappeared with the martini bottle, the ice bucket, a bowl of olives and a little gin in the small decanter. I mixed two drinks and indicated to him that he should take one. He looked unhappy.

'Well, Cecil?'

He sank his head.

'All right, then, if you won't play I shall go out. Bring me my umbrella and raincoat. I shall walk down the road and look at the girls. Are there girls out there, do you suppose?'

'Indeed there are.'

I could almost hear his mind ticking over the limits of his duties.

'One more thing, Cecil; my stick, I think.'

'Madam!' I could see his lip trembling as he approached with the raincoat held up for me to sleeve into and the umbrella hooked over his arm. 'Forgive me, Ms Fanshawe. I cannot help thinking this is unwise.'

'You are right, young man, it is most unwise. Stick!'

He placed his hand under my elbow but I knocked it away and hobbled off fairly satisfactorily with the aid of the little cherry cane.

'You have not been out of this house for six weeks, Ms Fanshawe. You haven't left the drawing room for the past four. You are not well and have been advised to stay in bed. It is an unusually filthy day. Have you not heard the storm?'

'Thank you, Cecil. I'll take the hat. Remind me to give you a rise. Close the door. I won't be watched along the path.'

I heard the lock engage behind me. The wind almost bowled me over before I caught hold of the rail which ran from the steps down the path to the street. It howled and whistled as clouds raced across the charcoal sky. Trees

131

creaked as they arced from side to side, their battered leaves rustling loud as traffic in my ears. In the distance I heard the sound of metal clattering onto the ground. I pulled my hat down as far as it would go.

Where is my blackbird hiding his sleek blue feathers and his yellow beak? I wondered. I've not been down this path since you went, one of those brief afternoons in November. Eleven years in two small suitcases. You didn't look back. It was raining then, too, but I felt you were smiling. Something told me you were walking out smiling, like a young woman going off to college. Where are you, darling? I could have put a bullet in your back. I could have watched you fold up on the concrete. Are you safe from the storm? Playing somewhere with your little girl in a fairytale house covered in ivy?

The gate swung wide as I unlatched it. I'd been using it for support and fell forward with it, landing on one knee and the top sections of those fingers which had been clutching the cane. I was quite immobilized. Cecil would have heard nothing through the noise of the storm and would not be able to see me if he chanced to look out unless he turned off the lights and concentrated for some time. I wondered if lightning might strike me but reassured myself: I was too low on the ground. I inched the stick out from under my fingers. The gate swung to and fro, clanging against my knuckles. I'd have to get up soon or pass out with the pain of it. I concentrated on garnering strength.

The brakes of a car screeched somewhere nearby and I heard a sharp thin voice: 'Can you hear me?' I couldn't answer; my mouth was clattering open and shut like a wooden puppet's, my tongue seemed to fill my whole mouth. Someone dragged me inside the car and arranged me in something like a sitting position. The light was switched on and I squeezed my eyes tight against it. The car was warm. I could drop off to sleep slumped here or could if I were not being shaken.

'Ms Fanshawe!'

I squinted one eye open a slit. 'Oh my god, Dr Bukowski!'

She had undressed her hair, or perhaps it had just fallen down. The effect was certainly rather different. I supposed a doctor's life could be strenuous.

'Ms Fanshawe. You are extremely lucky I was driving past. Are you quite mad?'

I let out a small snort. She was looking at me closely. 'Big breath out!' She lowered her nose towards my mouth. 'You've been drinking!'

She began to sound the horn while continuing to scrutinize me. I dropped my mouth onto hers. That would teach her. She didn't take her mouth away. She tasted like grapes and a little toothpaste. In fact, she tasted delicious.

'All right, Dr Bukowski,' I mumbled. 'Induce in me a little pleasure in the condition of life.'

There was a banging on the windscreen and I craned my head to see Cecil mouthing on the glass. Dr Bukowski opened my door and she and Cecil took my arms round their shoulders and escorted me indoors.

'Thank god you were there, Sally,' said Cecil when I was settled.

'Do you mean to say you know this woman?' I enquired.

'I do, madam, she's a friend of my sister's. She has been a regular visitor to my parents' home since we were all children.'

'Will you prepare a room for her?'

'I shall stay here in the drawing room with you, Ursula, until the sickness has passed.' She smiled at me, a spacious generous smile. Her make-up had faded and her skin shone through it.

'Come and sit beside me,' I said. 'I'm weak and shaken. Hold my hand.'

She came towards me and felt my forehead. 'Cecil, would you bring some iced water and a cloth?'

'Sally?' I said. 'Is that your name?'

'You couldn't pronounce my name.' She stroked my forehead.

I felt close to tears. 'Cecil,' I said, for he had not gone yet, 'would you be kind enough to take your friend next-door for a little while? Why don't you both have a drink; you deserve one.'

I am going to die, Elean, and you will rue your cruelty for the rest of your life. I will brief Cecil on the small black cards to send out for my funeral. Will she come, do you think, reader? Will she swoon with grief and remorse? Will the sobs break from her, slowly at first, then loud and heaving as if she'd vomit? Will she throw her slender body over the coffin as the first clay starts to fall from the spade?

I fear you are right. I shall be obliged to haunt her. I will roam your garden, Elean, and toxify your plants till they shrivel beneath the ground. I'll seep under your door-frames and flutter your curtains as you watch TV. I'll rattle the plates on your table, shatter the glass as you lift it to your mouth. I'll wake you and your little blonde lover at night with the bed hovering inches from the floor. I'll drive *you* to the doctor, Elean, I'll drive you to a shrink.

Cecil escorted Sally back into the drawing room and took his leave for the evening.

'Madam, I have made the doctor up a bed in the small bedroom.'

'Thank you, dear boy.'

She came and sat on the arm of the couch. I drummed my fingers lightly on the side table.

'Will you sleep with me, Sally?'

'I'd be delighted.'

She smiled and I took her palms to my lips.

Dr Bukowski remained for three days in the drawing room. I found I had no trouble maintaining the special diet she prescribed. Indeed, I doubt I have ever made such a speedy and efficient recovery from an indisposition. After those three days we both moved to my bedroom and she went back to work.

When two weeks were up, she suggested we celebrate with an expedition; she was emphatic. 'Did you, by any chance, receive an invitation to an extravaganza?' she asked.

'As it happens, I did. What on earth do you know about it?'

'Only that it'll be fun. We'll go, shall we?'

'Perhaps. Ask me nearer the time.'

On the morning itself, I agreed. I'd just been approached to do my first series of television programmes and was feeling rather sprightly. I called in my hairdresser. That evening I wore my best black gaberdine costume and filled it out rather better than I would have done for some while. Sally wore a loose blouse of strawberry silk, blue trousers and a small blue Turkish-style cap. It was a month now since she had first visited with her black bag and the elaborate maquillage she'd since abandoned.

She drove to a discreet club in a residential terrace in Islington where the doorwoman accepted our invitations and took our coats. We walked through to a surprisingly spacious double room lit in gentle rose patches by those little frosted-glass labial lights, and took a small table beneath one of them. Groups of rather elegant men sat at the other tables, and a few women dressed eccentrically enough to be fashion designers. A small ballroom orchestra played on the stage. Two male couples danced like Fred Astaire and Ginger Rogers on the floor.

At the signal of an extended soft drum roll, all the lights eclipsed and the curtains opened on a small stage lit pale green like a young meadow. Onto the boards glided a strange array of actors costumed and masked as animals, birds and butterflies. They danced very slowly while the music pulsed around them like a hot afternoon. I turned to Sally and she rested her head on my shoulder.

'Don't tell me this is the kind of entertainment favoured by today's girls,' I said, 'because I won't believe you.'

'No,' she said, 'this is special: doctor's orders.'

The floor lights started to rise and the orchestra struck up a waltz against the pulse of the performance tape. The dancers descended the steps from the stage and chose partners to take to the floor. Sally danced with a young eland. Watching them glide around the floor among the other couples, I felt a touch of pride in my young lover with her hand lightly on the pelted waist of her partner. She glanced from time to time in my direction. I am no dancer but I felt the rhythm lift something in my chest and hold me.

For my part, I was sorry when the pulse faded and the orchestra rolled their tune to a pretty diminuendo. The players made a brief reverence to their partners and ran to the stage to strike a final tableau as the curtains drew. The leader of the orchestra stepped up in a spotlight in front of them and announced a short interval before the next entertainment. I went to the bar and ordered our drinks. Two pleasant enough women asked me if I could

be Ursula Fanshawe. I smiled. 'Yes, I'm enjoying it enor-
mously,' I replied.

When the lights dimmed again, the orchestra started a
pastoral tune, flute, violins and oboe and the curtains drew
back to reveal a stage lit lilac. At the centre a slim figure
turned slowly. His dark curls falling across his well-
defined features put me in mind of a young Cretan about
to leap the bull. He wore nothing but bands of green fabric
barring his arms and legs and covering his loins. Each
time he turned, a small bird, a budgerigar or canary, fluttered from one of his hands and encircled the stage, until
there were thirty or forty of them, wheeling and arcing
over his head. At this point, the boy stood still, stretched
out his palms, and broke into song:

> Golden slumbers kiss your eyes
> Smiles awake you when you rise
> Sleep, pretty darling, do not cry
> And I will sing a lullaby.

By this time all the birds had flown onto him and perched
along his outstretched arms and head.

'Goodnight, ladies and gentlemen,' he said, 'and thank
you.'

'Well, Dr Bukowski, I think that would rank as one of
the seven daftest evenings in the history of my life.'

She looked concerned until I started laughing.

'God almighty, Sally, have I been awake for the last
couple of hours?'

'Yes,' she said. 'Have you been awake for the last
month?'

A cold shiver ran through my chest to the floor and
stayed there. I felt quite lightheaded. 'Shall we go dancing?' I said.

'Oh yes, let's!' She was giggling. 'What do you think of

our Cecil then?' She gave a little skip. 'I used to do an act with him.'

I opened my mouth and closed it again.

'If we ever get back to Bourne Hill,' I said, 'that boy is going to tell me about his family.'

Red Geraniums

Pushpa Sellers

That was the summer she started to eat geranium petals, the bright red ones, never the pink. She ate them because of their colour. They gave her strength. They made her blood flow strongly, healthily. She lay on the sofa and he came and sat at the other end, he lifted her feet gently onto his lap. The surrounding garden was bright and crisp. 'The glass makes it summer,' she said.

'It IS summer,' he replied. 'The sun's out and it's warm.'

'Only because we're all sending out good vibes today. We can control the weather by being positive. We can control anything through our collective concentration. We just need to realize it.'

'Don't be ridiculous. There's no way we can control the weather, no matter how hard we try,' he laughed.

'You see, it's people like you that keep it from happening. You shouldn't be so negative. All it takes is a bit of faith.'

She gathered herself up quietly and padded out to the garden in her bare feet. Her brown skin was shining against her loose red trousers, her arms were shimmering against her yellow shirt. She stood still, marvelling. She picked a geranium petal.

'Red is the colour of blood,' she said, returning to her

former position. She dropped the petal into her cup of herb tea. 'This cup is shimmering, it's so white.'

'You're turning into a geranium,' he said, smiling as he massaged her feet lightly, delicately.

Later that day she went around the house throwing things away; all the black things she put into the bin. 'Black is evil,' she kept whispering to herself. Black the colour of snakes and flies; stereos and TVs adding to the world's static; the black rubbish bags will keep the evil static from escaping. She threw away the milk and butter too. They looked dangerous, sitting treacherously in the fridge. They tried to look innocent but she could 'see' now and she saw right through them. She threw away her camera and her black perfume bottle. When she got her strength back she would throw away the big things; the stereo system and the television.

She opens drawers and lifts out all the dangerous things in there: her black jewellery, her Art Deco earrings and her black pearls, her black and white crystal necklace. She cleanses her wardrobe of black jumpers, skirts and shirts. She puts all these things into a black plastic bag and ties the opening up very tightly. There mustn't be any space for the static to get out. She drags it all down to a remote corner in the basement so that it will not contaminate the things around it.

A picture hangs above her bed. A red man and a blue woman. She sleeps under the red man and she is warm and content. She wakes up shivering and sees that she has rolled over and she is sleeping under the blue woman's gaze. She moves over to the red warmth. 'Protect me,' she whispers and falls into a peaceful sleep.

A butterfly waiting in the white room, she is at rest. She

will rest for a while and then in a blaze of colour she will emerge. She is enveloped in the pink light of sunshine filtered through the pink velvet curtains; womb-like. She awaits her moment. She counts to three and creeps out of bed. She chooses her clothes carefully. Blood-red trousers – an affirmation of her health – and a yellow shirt full of sunshine. It is midday and these are her middle of the day clothes. Earlier she wore orange and, jewel-like, she greeted the day. She descends and is given a cup of tea; brown and earth-like. She needs grounding and she gratefully accepts.

It is not long since her skin smelt of flowers and her breath had a sweet fragrance. She had been bleeding internally but when they cut her open the bleeding had ceased. Confused, they had cleaned up the four pints of blood and sewn her up again. They had cut her down the middle, from below her breasts to her pubis. They had cut straight through her naval and it was as though she had been reborn. She had lain for seven days, cocooned in swaddling clothes. And on the seventh night she had risen from her bed.

The flowers that her friends brought her were bright, almost luminous, and needed no attention. She was always the first to notice when the other patients' flowers were drooping and would immediately offer to freshen them up. She would change the water and lightly run her hands over the blooms and they would shine under her touch, restored to life. She would smile then, her radiant smile.

She was drawn instinctively to the women who needed her attention most. She would sit by them and listen, take their hands, and soon they would be telling her their inner-

141

most fears and allowing the tears that had been dammed up for so long to flow. She sat with those who were dying and willed them back to health. The doctors and nurses marvelled at the quick recovery rate of all the patients on this ward.

She had no need for sleep. Her life seemed a continual meditation. She would lie with her eyes open, a smile playing softly on her lips, listening to distant singing and to silent whisperings of the sea.

On the twelfth night she went to bed as usual having bid all her friends goodnight. She shut her eyes and thanked God for another wonderful day. It was then that she heard the voice. It was an unearthly sound like a voice from Hell itself. 'Choose,' it said.

She lay very still trying to ignore that she had heard it. The fragrance of flowers wafted over her, stronger and sweeter than ever before.

And then another smell that blotted out the first like a blanket, the foulest stench of death and decay, of wilting chrysanthemums and rotting flesh. She broke out into a cold sweat and shivered. She wanted to call out for help but she knew that there was no one that could help her now. The perfume of roses and geraniums washed over her again.

'Give me time,' she whispered.

But the voice was louder now and more insistent. 'Choose!' it commanded.

She saw her friends and husband, their decomposing flesh, their inevitable deaths and she knew that to choose this charmed existence would require commitment from her; a separation from her husband. She loved her husband too much, she could not bear to be parted from him. It would mean watching all her friends, her family disintegrate and die while she went on and on, lonely and timeless. With tears trickling down her cheeks she made her decision. Then, abruptly, as though a switch had been thrown, the fragrance of flowers was gone. There was only an overpowering smell of decay and death, the smell of sewers and rotting flesh. Suddenly the pain from her wound was intense. She watched as the rose petals darkened and shrivelled, the bright orange tiger lilies turned dull and crumpled. The tulips gaped and their withered petals floated gently to the floor, one by one.

She has accepted her fate now; there is no going back. She has lost her gift of life. And now all that she has to offer is this, the showering of colour.

Only Colouring-in

Linda Leatherbarrow

First there was a ballerina in trainers, then a drag artist with a mongrel in a diamanté collar, a juggler with a unicycle and, finally, a stand-up comic who read poems about spectacles.

After the show I noticed the juggler leaning against the bar, looking flat and tired and rolling a cigarette, so I told him how much I'd enjoyed his act.

'Did you?'

'I liked the Marx.'

While he'd thrown an assortment of quoits, pins and burning brands with his hands, his mouth had punched out a contraflow of political propaganda, tossing slogans into the babble and the smoke.

Now his voice was arch and mannered.

'How do you like my shoes? I don't wear them for every show. Just when I need some help.'

I smiled. They were wonderful. Cherry-red brothel creepers with thick crepe soles. They reminded me of a pair of scarlet ballet pumps I'd had when I was twenty, when I was at art school and worried about my image.

'Would you like a drink?' I offered.

'Let me. Mine come free.'

He leant over the bar and was served almost at once.

'Do you do it full-time?' I asked.

'Hardly anyone does it full-time. Wouldn't pay the rent. I do other stuff as well. A bit of script-writing for the telly. Comedy shows mainly. Occasionally I even get to act in them. Perhaps you've seen me?' I shook my head. 'I'm on and off pretty sharpish.' He smoked quietly for a moment then stubbed out his cigarette. 'I'm doing this children's book. Doing all the pictures myself. It's nearly killing me. Wish I'd never begun the bloody thing.'

'Perhaps you shouldn't have.'

He looked at me sharply and slid his voice into Cockney. 'I gotta keep the wolf from the door, babe.'

'You can't do anything without money.'

'I was on the dole once. Very dull.'

'*I'm* on the dole. I used to be an art teacher.' I wanted to add something more, something positive about welcoming the chance to develop my own work, but thought better of it.

'You poor thing!' he said brightly. 'You paint, though?'

I nodded.

'I so admire that. My book's just a comic. Not art at all. Perhaps you'd like to see it? You might be able to give me some pointers. Tell me where I'm going wrong.'

'I'd like to.'

'Good, that's lovely.' His voice made a final jump and in a public-school accent he said, 'Must dash now. People to meet, you know. Here's my card. Give me a ring sometime, whenever you feel like it, and pop round for a drink.'

He pecked at my cheek, a funny dry little kiss, very intimate coming from someone I'd only just met, and was gone, carried out of the crowd on his red shoes with his unicycle under one arm and his bag of juggling pins hanging from the other.

I must look like a good audience, I thought, swallowing

146

my drink and leaving. Someone had painted a white line down the middle of the pavement and I followed it as far as I could until it petered out on a bridge. It was a friendly sort of line and I was sorry to see it go.

I found his door next to an Italian delicatessen in Chapel Market and knocked on it once. Waited a long time. Wasps buzzed round shoppers too busy to notice, too intent on squeezing the tomatoes and avocados. The place had a curious earthy smell mixed up with the sharper one of rinds sweating in the sun and chip shop vinegar.

Just when I was about to give up, I heard footsteps coming down the stairs then the door opened and he stood there looking astonished.

'I was passing,' I lied, 'and wondered, if it wasn't inconvenient . . . if you'd like to show me your book?'

'Not at all. Absolutely delighted,' he said, recovering his poise. 'Do come in.'

I followed him up several flights of stairs past an insurance office on the first floor and a money lender's on the second. Even in the half-dark, it was clearly shabby and the juggler looked shabby too. He was wearing faded jeans, a felted mohair sweater and a pair of very down at heel black slippers, the sort you can buy in Chinese supermarkets. It seemed odd, on a hot day, to be wearing mohair but as I followed him up the stairs the house grew colder and colder. At the top was a bright pink door with a brass knocker.

'Welcome to my humble abode,' he said, unlocking the door with a brass key. 'Shall we go in?'

For a moment I hesitated.

He put the key back in his pocket.

'You never know who's around,' he said. 'There's always someone coming and going.' As if on cue, there were voices on the stairwell then a door slammed below us. 'I have to be careful.'

He pushed the door open with his toe and smiled at me. I couldn't decide if his eyes were blue or grey, just that they weren't brown. He had a deep cleft in his chin, otherwise it was a peculiarly ordinary face, the kind that would be hard to remember.

'You're thinking that I look like Harrison Ford. Now that I've mentioned it, don't you think I do? Lots of people have said so.'

'Can't see it myself,' I said, then added, 'perhaps a little.'

'After you.'

Again I hesitated, then saw he was flattered. It made him seem dangerous. I stepped in as boldly as I could.

The first room was a kitchen with a rickety table in the middle covered with various open jars of chutney and pickles, a carton of milk, and a bright blue earthenware coffee jug. It was a beautiful blue and it shone out of all the clutter like a clump of irises in a marsh. Near a window hung a row of shirts dripping steadily onto bare boards and beside them, next to an old-fashioned butler sink, stood an enamel bucket full of submerged clothes and steaming grey soapsuds.

'Just washing my grunts through when you knocked. Half a tic and I'll pour some coffee.'

I stood looking at the theatrical posters on the wall while he rinsed his hands and took down two mugs from a shelf. Zodiac mugs.

'Ghastly, aren't they?' he said. I gave a mock shudder and he flashed me a smile. 'My sister gave them to me. I'm so glad you called,' the voice distinctly public-school. 'I was having one of my domestic days and it's such a joy to be rescued.'

148

He poured me a large mug of black coffee and disappeared through a bead curtain.

'Do come through.'

I helped myself to milk from the carton and followed, pushing aside the strings of beads with my free hand. Very sixties, I thought, then nearly tripped over a saucepan strategically placed to catch a drip from the ceiling. It was a narrow room smothered in papers and drawing boards. A television winked in a corner – some ancient black and white movie. Women in padded shoulders mincing around, giving their menfolk a hard time, one of them toting a derringer. Mesmeric stuff.

'I like to have the telly on when I'm home,' he said. 'It's company. I always have it on when I work. Stops me going mad. I hate doodling around up here all by myself.'

He handed me a stack of finished artwork, very brightly coloured, predominantly in pinks and oranges, yellow and magenta.

'Really only colouring-in,' he said.

I could see that children would love it. It was about a man who did conjuring tricks with animals, who was a hopeless magician and completely dependent on the goodwill of the animals for the success of his show. It was beautifully drawn; I told him so and he was delighted. He was easy to please and I liked him, though, up close, in the daylight, he was a bit frayed about the edges. But then so was I.

Beside an iron grate and wedged into an acid-green alcove was a rail festooned with his stage clothes: zoot suits, dinner jacket, waistcoats, and, above them on a shelf, a big brimmed soft felt hat. He saw me eyeing it and put it on.

'Now say I don't look like Harrison Ford. Adventurer,

explorer and rescuer of maidens! Are you a maiden that needs to be rescued?'

'Maybe I am,' I said. I didn't like myself being coy.

He came closer. Underneath the exuberance of his hat his face looked suddenly peaky. His eyes wrinkled up in an expression half of pain, half-defiance.

'I'm a bit of an old roué.'

'You don't look it. Old roués don't wash their grunts and watch telly in the afternoon.'

'Ah, but that's *exactly* what they do. They just don't usually get caught doing it.'

He took the hat off then threw it hard against a sofa. It landed on a pile of discarded clothes and slithered onto the floor.

'I'm getting tired of it all. Used to think it was wonderful. Put the hat on, put the red shoes on, go out, do the juggling, go to a party, get smashed, get stoned, get laid, but it's beginning to go sour on me. I keep bumping into the same people, expecting me to be funny, expecting me to be randy.'

I had one of those self-conscious moments when you seem to be outside yourself. I was curled into a chair by his table with my hands clasped protectively round my knees. I saw how defensive I looked, how prim, how I'd chosen a chair that kept the table between us.

'I have to go.'

'Must you? It's been so nice showing you my things and if you go I shall have to work.'

'I ought to be working too.'

'Oh dear,' he sighed. 'Boring.'

I smiled.

'I do hope you'll come again,' he said, lifting his eyebrows.

He got a lot of mileage out of his eyebrows.

'Yes, I'd like to.'

Very briefly our eyes touched, then he stood up and bent towards me and kissed my cheek.

'I'll let myself out.'

I shook his hand and backed out of the room. As I ran down the stairs he must have turned the television up. A string orchestra played in a frenzy, lush and punctuated with gun shots.

I didn't go back for a week but it was a week in which I couldn't work and in which my room seemed unbearably lonely. On Monday evening I phoned him. I wasn't sure if it was fair. I told myself he only interested me as a friend, which should have been fine except I had a feeling that he had a little more in mind. Maybe I was the vain one. I wasn't sure about anything – I just couldn't bear another evening on my own. My best friend was in New York doing a course in media studies, another was in Crete with her boyfriend, and the rest had all got married and moved out of London and changed in the way that married people do.

I had a bath, washed my hair and dressed, putting on a heavy pink linen coat and sticking a black ostrich feather in the buttonhole. It was theatrical and extravagant, not at all in keeping with my mood.

'You look wonderful,' he said. 'I shall wear my hat.'

We went to a pub round the corner and he talked about bit parts in movies and name-dropped minor television personalities. We played Bowie and Roxy Music; there was nothing newer on the juke box. Afterwards, I went home in a taxi. I couldn't afford it but it went with the ostrich feather.

He got to be a habit over the next few weeks. Sometimes he came round to me and sometimes I went over to Islington. I'd completely given up the idea of working. My pictures were hidden in a portfolio because they seemed a reproach. I might as well get a job, I thought, if this doesn't stop. But I knew I wouldn't, not yet.

One night in his room, a hot night when the windows were wide open and the city ground and screeched outside like a cat miaowing at a mouse hole, I sat down on his sofa and he came at once and sat next to me, as though he'd been waiting for me to sit there for a long time. He had, too, because from the first I'd kept to the chair by the table.

He put his arm cautiously round my shoulder and pulled me towards him. At least half of me wanted to leave at once but we kissed and suddenly I wanted him to touch me, wanted to be close to somebody, up tight, naked, with anybody, I didn't care at all, just so long as I could be wrapped up out of all that anxiety and loneliness.

We undressed and went to bed and I made love to him as much as he made love to me. I wanted him but he kept slipping out of me and I kept losing him. I saw myself in a muddle of limbs and sweat and dirty sheets, in the centre of a room full of cigarette butts, cold coffee cups and empty beer cans; a stale room opening out onto a stale street full of rubbish and rotting fruit.

He lay for a while with his head against my breast, his breath hot on my skin, then raised himself on his elbows; I noticed for the first time that his eyes were green. His hair flopped over them and he smiled through it. I put my hand up and pushed it back. Thin, silky hair, recently hennaed for one of his brief television appearances.

'You're very tender,' he said. 'Not many women are these days, but you are.'

I was full of a muddled feeling I couldn't sort out, a feeling of being part of something impossibly fragile,

152

unbearably complex. I loathed myself for just letting things happen.

His arm was round me and he wanted me to stay the night. It was late and would have meant a taxi so I curled up against his side and tried to go to sleep. He fell asleep quickly but I lay awake most of the night. For some reason the sky was full of helicopters, police helicopters, chuntering backwards and forwards.

In the morning I woke to a foul-tasting mouth and itching eyes. The man lying next to me seemed extraordinary and improbable. I looked at his short hair on the pillow and the crumpled face beneath it and wanted to be out of there. I touched his face to wake him.

'I have to go now,' I said, sitting up and looking for my clothes, but his eyes opened up into mine and looked pleased and happy to see me there. He brought his hand out from under the sheet and began to stroke the skin over my shoulder bone in little delicate moves with his fingertips.

'Where's the fire? Wait a moment while I wake up then I'll make you breakfast before you go. It's early yet.'

He reached out with his other hand and manoeuvred an alarm clock into a position where he could read it.

'Surely you don't need to rush off this second?'

Beneath the window the market people were setting up their stalls, greeting each other, joking and swearing as they unloaded their vans. A cheerful noise. Beside me, he was rolling a cigarette and presently smoking it, coughing and tapping the ash over the side of the bed into an empty cup.

'What d'ya fancy for yer breakfast? There's the deli next-door. I could nip down and be back in a jiffy. Eggs? Sausages? Bacon?'

'Just toast, thanks. How come you're Cockney one minute and old school tie the next?'

'Habit, I suppose. When I went to boarding school I did the Cockney for a laugh but they took it seriously so I kept it up.'

'How long were you there?'

'Four years.'

'And you didn't once drop out of it?'

'It seemed a shame to disappoint them.'

He blew a smoke ring carefully into the morning and I watched it drift towards the window. When he'd finished his cigarette he swung his legs over the side of the bed and wrapped himself in a dressing gown that might have come from a Noël Coward play; silk, paisley and tassels. I heard him grinding coffee beans as I dressed and wrenched a comb through my hair. There was a heap of coins on a bamboo table by his bed. I jingled it in my hands and he heard me.

'That's busking money. One of these days I'll take it down the bank and get it changed. I usually wait till my sister comes round with her kids. I get them to count it into bags and give them a fiver for doing it – keeps them happy and it saves me the trouble. Your toast's ready.'

I went through and poured myself some coffee and nibbled at the toast. That morning the blue coffee jug was surrounded by little cartons, houmous and taramasalata and gentleman's relish.

'No wonder you're so skinny,' he said. 'Another slice?'

'No thanks. I've been a bit off my food lately.'

'Oh, I don't mind, darling.' He used the word carefully, self-consciously, as though testing it out. 'I don't mind at all. I think you're lovely, like a dancer.'

I ate his toast as fast as politeness allowed and drank down his coffee, scalding my tongue. It was good coffee,

154

fragrant and rich, but it might just as well have been instant. I didn't want him calling me darling and I didn't want him sitting opposite me in his dressing gown with his legs sticking out, bony and hairy, his face jumping around a little too quickly, and his forehead damp with sweat. There was a window behind him and the light hit the back of his ears and curled over the rims, a snail trail round each lobe. He raised his hand and smoothed his hair and smiled at me. You can't make love to a man one minute and want to run away from him the next, I thought, but that was exactly how I felt. I wanted to be out in the sunshine, feeling it on my skin, rushing along.

'Did I tell you I'm going to be a father?'

'No.'

'Part of my old roué phase. I told you it had gone sour on me.'

'I'd no idea.'

'Neither did I till a few weeks ago.'

It seemed to be sympathy he wanted but I felt shocked at the bitterness in his voice, distanced and unable to respond.

'It was just some woman I met at a party. I vaguely knew her. Friend of a friend in the business, bit of an actress. We had a quickie behind the tool shed. All I remember about it is her bottom bouncing up and down in the grass, very white. I don't even remember if I enjoyed it. I found out a few weeks ago she's pregnant so I went round to see her. Turns out she wanted to have a child and she used me to get one. I was drunk and we did it. That's all. It was nothing and now she's pregnant.'

'How do you know you're the father?'

'I don't but she says I am. It could have been anyone I expect but it had to be muggins. I wish she'd never told me.' He pulled his dressing gown tighter and crossed his

155

arms. 'I wonder if it'll look like me. I suppose I'll know for sure when it's born. It's bound to look a bit like me . . . or someone in the family. I think you'd recognize your own child, don't you?'

I nodded.

'I wish the bitch had never said anything and I'd never found out. She doesn't want me to have anything to do with it. After I'd got over feeling angry, I began to think about the child, my child. I offered to pay her bills and help with money but she insists on being independent. So here I am, going to be a father, and not even going to know my own child. It hurts, it really hurts.'

For once his face was still. He sat staring at the coffee jug with his mouth slightly twisted and his eyes far away. I knew it was selfish but I wanted to escape more than ever. I put out my hand and touched his arm for a moment.

'Look,' I said, 'I'm sorry, I really am. Very sorry about all this. I can see how you must feel but I don't know what to say. I lost a child once. It died before it was born. Perhaps this is sort of like that. I don't think about it much any more.'

He didn't seem to hear me.

'I can't handle this right now,' I said. 'I feel all used up. I'm going home. I'm sorry not to be more help.' I stood up. 'Thanks for the breakfast.'

'That's okay.'

'And for being nice last night.'

I said the last bit because he looked so forlorn.

'Will you come again?'

'Yes, of course,' I said. But I knew I wouldn't.

Six months later I met him on the platform at Kings Cross.

'It was a little boy,' he said. 'I knew he was mine as soon as I saw him.'

156

'Congratulations. I'm glad you got to see him.'

'I worked on her. I kept going round and offering to help out. She let me decorate her flat and I bought her a pram.'

'Will she let you have access?' I asked then wished I hadn't because his face screwed up and I thought he was going to cry.

'He kept having fits, turning blue. She doesn't even go to see him. He's in a special hospital and I don't think he'll ever come out. I go as often as I can but he doesn't know me. He doesn't know anyone.'

He took my hand and I looked down at the track. A mouse was whiskering a sweet wrapper.

'I saw your book,' I said, 'in the bookshops. It looked great.'

He shrugged disparagingly, then smiled in spite of himself. 'Are you still painting?'

'I do arts admin now. I'm arranging a photography exhibition.'

I sent him an invitation for the opening night and he turned up in a pale yellow suit. People were gulping down the free Lambrusco but he was distant and sober. I looked over the heads at him and felt a curious panic. I wanted to busy myself, trot round with the drinks, smile, and keep occupied, but I didn't. I thought of all the times I'd jumped into things and then jumped out again, quickly, too quickly, run away even. I thought, maybe we won't really get on, but that didn't seem to matter. The point was to start going up to people with the hand firmly held out, to stop, as it were, always having my hands in my pockets; like a kid, awkward, embarrassed, and not sure how to behave. What does it matter, I thought, if it doesn't work out? At least give it a try.

He was staring at a sunset photo.

'Horrendous, isn't it?' I said.

'Oh absolutely.'

I took his arm and we left. We walked along a canal towpath, under bridges, beneath trees, until we came to a park where a man was wheeling a bicycle. When we got closer we saw he had a chicken in the saddlebag. He lifted the chicken out and took it for a walk across the grass. When we left the park he was running, whistling and calling, and the chicken was racing ahead of him, its claws springing on the turf.

About the Authors

Christina Dunhill is a writer and freelance editor. *The Boys in Blue*, Women's Challenge to the Police, was published by Virago in 1989. Her stories have also been published in *Wild Hearts* (Sheba, 1991). She hopes to have a collection of her own stories published and is working on a novel. She teaches creative writing, and also a literature course on magic realism at the City University. She lives in Stoke Newington with one cat and is looking for a butler.

Frances Gapper's stories have appeared in *Time Out, Everywoman* and *Horticulture Week* magazines and in several anthologies. Her novel *Saints and Adventurers* was published by the Women's Press in 1988. She has also written a children's novel, *Jane and the*

Kenilwood Occurrences (Faber, 1979) and is co-author, with Patience Gapper and Sally Drury, of the _Blue Guide, Gardens of England_ (A&C Black, 1991).

Andie Hawthorn was born in 1953 and spent her childhood in England and Germany. She worked as a shop assistant, secretary, turkey inseminator, nurse and counsellor before reading English at Goldsmiths' College. She plays the guitar and has written poetry and songs. Her poetry has been published in _Spare Rib_. She lives and writes in Hackney and has two young children.

Linda Leatherbarrow's short stories have been published in magazines including _Writing Women_ and _Cosmopolitan_ and have also been broadcast on the radio; in 1987 she won first prize in the Wandsworth All London Literary Competition. She has worked as an illustrator, graphic designer, Sainsbury's shelf stacker, children's clothes designer, market stall holder and publisher of private press books. Now she works in a library in North London and has just finished writing a novel. She has three grown-up children.

About the Authors

Helen Sandler has a story for teenagers in Livewire's *School Tales* and another story in *Wild Hearts*, a collection of lesbian melodrama (Sheba, 1991). A 24-year-old displaced Mancunian, she lives with one of the other contributors to this book. She can swim 50 lengths of Tottenham Green baths, in either of two delightful costumes, with her goggles on.

Pushpa Sellers was born in Sri Lanka in 1954 of Indian parents. She spent her first eighteen years in Japan but has travelled extensively since then, studying and working in Bombay, Beirut, Belgium and North Yemen. She finally settled in England in 1973 where she was diagnosed as having Systemic Lupus Erythematosis which has led to kidney failure. She now lives in Stoke Newington with her English husband, writing and waiting for a transplant. (B kidneys welcome!) She has contributed to a collection of women's writing, *The Likes of Us*.

About the Authors

Robyn Vinten was born in 1961 and grew up in New Zealand, coming to England in 1986 in search of the bright lights. She works as an optician, attends acting classes and is involved in 'Slip of the Tongue' Theatre group. She also plays football for Hackney Women's Football Club. This is her first published story and she would like to thank her writing group for all their support and encouragement.

Wendy Wallace was born in 1956 and trained as a journalist. She spent most of the 1980s living in Egypt and the Sudan. She wrote and produced photographs for development booklets including *Praying for Rain, Facing the Future* and *Two Mothers*. Now living in London with her partner and two young sons she has had one short story published in *Iron Women* and is working, on a novel.